THEY DON'T MAKE PEOPLE LIKE THEY USED TO

Olden Times in Telfair County, Georgia

by Addie Garrison Briggs

MM John Welda BookHouse

2012

Published in 2012 by MM John Welda BookHouse
P.O. Box 111, Eastman, Georgia 31023

ISBN: 978-0-9839365-8-9 (Hardcover)
LCCN: 2012955545
The Lightwood History Collection: Book 6
A Revised and Expanded Edition of the original book
First published 1985 by Addie Garrison Briggs and Elspeth Enterprises

Cover Photograph of the Levy Garrison and Lydia Hulett Garrison Family taken circa 1901, courtesy Nell Davis Harris

This book is dedicated

To

My Father, L. Saxton Garrison, Sr.

who

Gave me a love of history

And to

My Husband, William J. Briggs

who

Encouraged me to write it down

The author's father, Levy Saxton Garrison, Jr. (1908-2001)
and Cuthbert, the goat.
Saxton always wanted to name something Cuthbert
and the goat did not object.

CONTENTS

True Tales, Slightly Embroidered
A Prologue

Rembert Cravey, his wife Marianne, and their two children had a habit of attending Sunday evening church services at Mt. Zion Methodist Church near Milan, Georgia, then going up the road a piece to Uncle Bob's front porch where they enjoyed his stories.

One night on the way back home, Marianne asked: "Rembert, your Uncle Bob's stories—Do you reckon they are really true?"

"I don't know whether they are or not," Rembert replied. "But either way, they're still mighty good stories."

Irish storytellers have the gift of taking an actual fact, and like adding harmony to a basic tune, or embroidering a garment, they change things just enough so that the finished product is more pleasing to the senses than the original fact .

My father, Saxton Garrison, Sr., was my source for most of the stories in this book. True to his many Irish genes, he could embroider with the best of them.

An Introduction
by Stephen Whigham

Addie Garrison Briggs first published *They Don't Make People Like They Used To* in 1985. The original, hardcover edition sported a handsome red cover with its title stamped in gold lettering on the front. Her lively book with the bold, declarative title enjoys an impressive local reputation nearly three decades after it first appeared. Her tales—some of them 'tall' tales, by her own description—run the gamut from humor to tragedy, from pathos to the inspiration of family life. All of them draw from the well of family relations and community, recounting a way of life and culture perhaps dim and unrecognizable in our modern age.

Ms. Briggs spent many years honing her writing skills to bring forth this entertaining collection of family stories. The stories take place in the south Georgia area in and near Milan, of Telfair County, Georgia and the surrounding locale. This area is located approximately 175 miles south of Atlanta and 150 miles west of Savannah. Her stories cover a period from as far back as the early 1800's. She writes of ancestors from Massachusetts, including family from the town of Salem, of witchcraft fame.

The history of the south Georgia area following the Civil War interweaves with the arrival of the Northern timber companies. Prior to the Civil War, the area was quite remote, referred to by one historian as the "inner frontier." Railroads opened up the area bringing settlers to new towns and hamlets to harvest the primeval pine forests of the "pine barrens." The area near Milan became the location of one of the larger sawmills, originally called Camp Six. Farmers and herders, such as Ms. Briggs' ancestors, already lived in the area. Some of them, along with their neighbors, became entangled in land disputes with the timber concerns. Several of the stories in her book recount this history. Murder, betrayal, and disappointment stemmed from these epic clashes. Yet the Garrisons and their relations carried on the fight.

Part I of this new edition of Addie Garrison Briggs book includes several new stories. Among her many skills as a writer, Ms. Briggs displays a particular genius creating titles for her stories.

Part II of the book covers the family history and genealogy of the Garrisons, Williams and related families. Ms. Briggs encourages interested readers and family researchers to contact her if they seek further information.

The reader will note that the author and publisher made every effort to provide quality photographs for this edition. We made decisions to use some photographs based on their rarity and importance to this work, compromising on the perfect quality in the search for completeness in the historical record.

They Don't Make People Like They Used To is Book 6 in the series known as The Lightwood History Collection. Included in this series are the works of area novelist Brainard Cheney, whose novels address the timber wars and other events covering the period from 1820 through 1945. The publisher plans to release additional series titles in the future.

THEY DON'T MAKE PEOPLE LIKE THEY USED TO

Caution: Read Before Proceeding Further

Contrary to what one often reads in local histories and genealogies, our ancestors were not all saints. Neither were they all war heroes and most of them were far more likely to struggle along on a small farm than to own a large plantation. In short, one might say that our forebears failed to live up to our expectations.

We have built molds designed by our romantic desires of what we would like our ancestors to have been. Such flawless molds they are. But alas! That stubborn great–grandfather simply won't fit into his mold. And that certain great-aunt, what's the matter with the woman? Doesn't she know that she should stand taller in this respect; and that she shouldn't be so prominent in this area?

The trouble with these ancestors was that they were real people. Sometimes they were good, sometimes bad; sometimes they were wise, and sometimes foolish. Perhaps they were a bit like us, with one major difference. There seems to have been more of a spirited quality to their lives. Whatever a man's actions, whether funny, tragic, or decidedly wicked, he did it with a definite dash. Therefore, while their lives may embarrass us, they will at the same time unquestionably intrigue us.

PART ONE:
STORIES

Lucius Lazarus Williams and his second wife, Margaret McDermid.
Lucius Williams was murdered during the Dodge Land Wars.
(Photograph courtesy of Julian Williams)

Fighting

Polly Ann Garrison was furious. Two red-faced, sweating men circled, punched, tangled, and rolled in her yard. The combatants were her brother, Levy Garrison, and her husband, Jesse Jones.

"Stop it!" she commanded, stomping her foot on the pine floor of the porch. "You should both be ashamed. Two grown men, fighting over a DOG."

"Shut up, Polly Ann," her brother panted. "We had just as soon fight about a dog as anything else!"

In this part of the country, there has always been a lot of fighting. Fights about dogs and fights about women. There have been fights about cursing and fights about prayers. And impulsive fights and fights with malice aforethought. Some of the results have been tragic and some humorous.

The first of the battles in this section were, of course, the Indian wars, which, distanced by time, now seem thrilling. At the time they happened, they were considered a dangerous and bloody nuisance.

Then there was THE WAR. Everybody who was anybody attended that one. Of course, it took place "off up yonder". And only a few stray Yankees wandered through this section, begetting a child here and there.

Many wars, little and big, are fought over the possession of land. So it was with our biggest fight down here. With one major difference, our homegrown war, with its varied and colorful battles, was pitched over territory that, in the first place, nobody had wanted.

Most early Georgians preferred living along the rivers, and turned up their collective noses at the uplands. The wild pinelands between the Oconee and Ocmulgee Rivers were disdainfully referred to as the "pine barrens." And some people wouldn't have that land as a gift. In fact, when the state of Georgia sought to grant title to potential settlers by means of a land lottery, there were very few takers. Thrown back to the state, two hundred and seventy-five thousand acres of this timberland was subsequently granted to Peter J. Williams of Milledgeville. If those first awarded the land could have foreseen the future, their tastes would almost certainly have been different. For this timberland, along with an additional twenty-five thousand acres later acquired by Williams, was the prize which launched a battle lasting into the twentieth century.

Although the trouble did not begin until the 1870's, the seeds of conflict were sown long before the civil war.

In 1835, the Williams land was sold to Colby, Chase and Crocker, agents for a Maine land association. Promoters of this group, with visions of making a fortune in the timber market, formed the Georgia Lumber Company; and all the newly acquired lands were conveyed to that corporation. What was said to be the largest sawmill in the southeast was put into operation, and the colony which grew up around the mill was known as Lumber City.

But the venture was not successful; the lumber company went broke; and the lands were abandoned. However, before its demise, the corporation had mortgaged the property to the State of Indiana. So Indiana became the owner of five hundred square miles of Georgia.

Apparently she thought little of her acquisition, for she failed to pay the county taxes on the land. Meanwhile, Telfair County residents were having second thoughts about the desirability of the land. So, when Telfair County's Tax Commissioner, James Boyd, held a tax sale, there were hundreds of takers. The lots, selling for as little as six cents each, included, not only land in Telfair County, but also in a good share of present-day Dodge County.

Ignoring such transactions, Indiana, after having retained title for nine years, sold these same lots, along with the rest. The title passed through several hands, while settlers, both with and without tax deeds, were in actual possession of the land.

In 1868, William Eastman obtained a deed to the three hundred thousand acres. In that same year, he, along with A.G.P. Dodge, William Chauncey, and others, incorporated the Georgia Land and Lumber Company. Under the presidency of William E. Dodge, they hoped to develop the timber resources on a grand scale. Construction was started on miles of tramroads to transport the huge logs from forests to sawmills located on the Macon and Brunswick Railroad. And many logs were to be rafted down the rivers to the Darien market. In addition, big distilleries were built for the production of turpentine.

Many Georgians welcomed the coming of the Yankee capitalists. In 1870, a new county was created and named for Dodge. Its seat of government was named for William Eastman. And a village bears the name of Chauncey.

Those living in the pine woods felt differently. Much of this land was now occupied. And the residents intended to stand their ground. The tax deeds were dated 1845, and Georgia law stated that undisturbed occupancy for seven years cleared a disputed title. And for those deedless settlers, there was the law which based ownership on twenty years undisturbed occupancy, even without color of title. And, of course, there were the newcomers who determined to stay on the land by dint of a 'coffee-pot' deed and/or shotgun. (Coffee-pot deeds were those which had been soaked in coffee to give the appearance of age.)

The Georgia Land and Lumber Company, as a foreign corporation, (not incorporated in Georgia,) appealed directly to the federal courts. And in 1876, tax sales to Josiah Paine and several others were declared void.

The next year the Georgia Legislature passed an act requiring all foreign corporations with more than five thousand acres of Georgia land

3

to incorporate under local state law. Rather than do this, the Georgia Land and Lumber Company transferred all its lands to George E. Dodge. But development of the property was still carried on by the corporation.

Many of the settlers were still sticking tight to the land. And, in efforts to evict them, Dodge was forced to resort to state courts. Cases tried locally were invariably won by those occupying the land. This was partly due to the ability of a colorful lawyer, Luther A. Hall, whose eye patch won him the name "Leather Eye." But no one doubted that the success of local claimants was due in large part to juries made up of fellow settlers.

Then Hall thought he had found an even better way to defeat the Dodge Company. In court, Mr. Dodge had relied on what was called his "short chain of title." This was based on a separate deed which William Eastman had obtained from the heirs of the original owner, Peter J. Williams. It was upon the validity of this later deed that the Dodge Company was depending. Thanks to Oliver Briggs, a clerk in Dodge's land office, Hall discovered why Dodge was so reluctant to use his first chain of title. The document conveying title from Colby, Chase, and Crocker to the old Georgia Lumber Company had never been recorded.

Hall, Briggs, Silas Butler, and Henry Sleeper, reasoning that this failure did not invalidate the deeds to Colby, Chase and Crocker, rushed to buy the disputed lands from the heirs of those three gentlemen. Then, opening a land office, they advertised lots of land at low prices and on liberal terms. Buyers poured into the office.

This action nicely weakened Dodge's short chain of title. But it placed the conflict back in the jurisdiction of the federal court. In 1886, Hall's land office sales were declared invalid. And he, along with his associates, was enjoined from further interfering with Dodge's possession of the disputed lands.

But the settlers were quite adept at interfering. Gunslinging was not a neglected art in these parts. And sniping at timber cutters was popular. Burning of tramroads was also widely practiced.

It was all to no avail. Not only had the Yankee court spoken, but the timber company had a few hired guns of its own. So the Dodge Company pressed relentlessly on, harvesting the virgin pine products.

Then a few very determined settlers came up with a "better" idea. They reasoned that the murder of a company agent would terrorize Dodge into making some concessions. John Forsyth was the chosen victim; and Rich Lowery, a North Carolinian of mixed Indian, Negro, and white blood, was hired for the job. The latter was promised six hundred dollars upon successful completion of the deed.

Since Lowery did not know Forsyth by sight, one of the conspirators arranged to engage Forsyth in a pleasant conversation on a Chauncey street. He gave the intended victim a friendly pat on the arm; and Lowery, standing off a short distance, knew the face of his prey.

Six nights later, Forsyth was at home with his wife and family in the village of Normandale, near Chauncey. Sitting in an easy chair, smoking an after-dinner cigar, he was unaware of a dark figure peering through the window. Then gunshots tore into the room. And young Nellie Forsyth, upon seeing her father fall, ran out into the rainy night for a physician. But within a few hours John Forsyth was dead.

A month passes and the identity of the killers was unknown. Then a relative of one of them casually gave the details of the scheme to what he considered a sympathetic ear. But the listener had no stomach for murder and turned the information over to a Dodge agent.

True bills against ten men were returned by the grand jury of the United States Circuit Court. But not all of them were brought to trial. Henry Lancaster was indicted but never arrested. The day after Forsyth's murder, Andrew Renew was gunned down by a Dodge posse which was attempting to trail the killers. He was indicted posthumously.

5

Rich Lowery also escaped trial. Some reported that, with the blood money in his pocket, he had disappeared into a thicket and was never accounted for again. But whispers among relatives and neighbors of his employers told a different story.

The scheme has been to obtain the blood money pledged from interested parties. But why pay out the money when you don't have to? Surely no one was expected to sue for collection. So some of the pledges were not met; and Rich Lowery was given three hundred dollars and asked to wait two weeks for the rest.

Looking around his circle of employers, he growled, "Nobody said nothing about waiting. I killed once for that money, and I'll do it again if I have to. I'll give you—"

But he never finished his threat, because, as soon as his attitude became evident, one man slipped behind him, fat pine limb in hand. And when Rich Lowery was dead, his body was thrown into the black waters of a cypress swamp.

The trial began on December 8, 1890, in Macon, Georgia. The court room was crowded. One hundred and forty witnesses were present. Four hundred jurors had been called. Friends and relatives of the defendants had come from five counties.

The defendants, sitting in a group, were not all together in spirit. The very ill Lem Burch, who had suffered a stroke soon after the murder, had pled guilty and turned state's evidence. He was able to be in the courtroom only on the first day of the trial and spent the rest of the ordeal in a boarding house bed across the street.

Counsel for Wright and John Lancaster, James Moore, Luther Hall, and Lewis Knight attempted to have their clients tried separately from Charlie Clements, who sat glowering at his former partners. Those lawyers contended that the interests of their clients were not the same as those of Clements. Their reasons were very good, even if all of them were not stated in court.

Clements had allegedly actually been present at the murder. And a story had been circulated that he had been an unwilling participant in the conspiracy. He had been, so the rumor went, in serious trouble with the law. Wright Lancaster, Telfair County sheriff, had been assisting Clements' efforts to stay out of jail. Now it seemed that the young Telfair County Sheriff wanted a favor in return. Lancaster, who was himself deeply involved in the land troubles, and whose own father had been killed by a Dodge Company woodsman, had dirty work for Charlie to do. That job entailed supervising the elimination of a very valued Dodge Company employee. Clements, it seemed, had a choice—he could help the sheriff or go to jail. And it was hinted that perhaps his fate could even be worse than a jail sentence.

But the defense attorney's pleas for a separate trial were as unrewarding as had been their attempts to have the trial removed from federal court on the grounds that only state courts have jurisdiction in a murder case.

Finally, with days of unsuccessful defense motions over, the trial began in earnest. Witnesses were sworn in and weeks of testimony began, both in the courtroom and at the bedside of Lem Burch.

Nellie Forsyth was expected to be a very important witness. Her description of her father's death would give dramatic emphasis to the case of the prosecution. Coming into the courtroom, she felt ill at ease among so many men and chose a seat beside two young girls. They happened to be the motherless daughters of one of the prisoners. This unwittingly pointed out the tragedy of innocent victims on both sides of the legal fence.

Nellie's testimony did have its impact. And after a lengthy and emotion-packed trial, only one of the defendants escaped conviction. James Moore was acquitted on all charges. Luther Hall, Wright Lancaster, and Charlie Clements were found guilty as charged and given life sentences. Louis Knight and John Lancaster were found guilty of conspiracy only and were sentenced to six year terms.

One other Telfair County man also went to the Ohio State Penitentiary, although he had absolutely nothing to do with the conspiracy to murder. Rube White spent several years raising geraniums in the prison flower house alongside Luther Hall. For, in the course of their search for the murderers, the authorities had inadvertently discovered Rube's liquor still.

The murder trial was over, but the court suits seemed everlasting. Such was the hatred generated by all aspects of the land war, that for twelve years prior to 1907, the name of no man in Laurens, Telfair, or Dodge Counties was placed in the jury boxes of the United States Court in Macon. Not overly impressed with the moral character of its residents, agents of the federal government treated the whole area as "outlaw country".

It was not until 1923, that the United States Court system was finally finished with the Dodge litigation. By then the vast timber resources had already been harvested from the Dodge forests. In fact, the last of the cut-over lands had been in other hands for several years.

The timber company had, through the years, maintained a policy of letting peaceable settlers buy the land even while the timber was being removed.

And land possessed by one of the more warlike residents was once offered for sale even before its timber harvest had begun. A certain Mr. Cannon, recently moved from Pennsylvania, was approached by a Dodge agent with the tempting offer of several lots of land, forested with trees many of which were six feet in diameter. The price was "very reasonable," which, of course, is another way of saying "cheap".

Mr. Cannon, with an eye to looking over the property, approached a house where a brawny, bearded man lounged on the porch. Upon introducing himself, Mr. Cannon inquired about the land.

"This here is my land," drawled the settler, rising to about six feet four.

"When did you buy it?"

"I didn't. Pa gave it to me."

"Would you be interested in selling?"

"Nope. Don't ever intend getting rid of it," the big man replied, reaching casually for his rifle.

Whereupon, Mr. Cannon made a quick decision. He concluded that this particular piece of property was not quite what he had in mind. The price was a tad too high.

One peaceable Telfair county resident got full possession of his land without a fight or a price. David Cravey Jr., knowing well that his land title was uncertain, had early-on approached the Dodge Company with a proposal. He had already cleared the best tillable land and was farming it. He asked for—and got—a lease to continue farming, while the company, without interference, could cut the remaining timber.

But the trees were not cut quickly enough. What was worse, the lease had not been recorded, but had been unwisely left in the care of the local justice of the peace, who was a relative of the farmer. When that official died in the fall of 1885, the Dodge Company agents remembered that lease and rode speedily to the home of the deceased.

But two of the late justice's older sons had already gone through their father's effects. Not liking the looks of the aforementioned legal paper, they had promptly burned it.

The Dodge Company now had no evidence that there had ever been a lease. Cravey had been in peaceful possession of that land for over seven years since the arrival of the timber company. It would appear that the Dodges weren't even claiming this particular tract. So they decided to let this one go.

Nearly seventy years have passed since the powerful timber company let the last of their lands pass out of their hands. Today most of the children growing up between the Ocmulgee and Oconee rivers have never heard of the Dodge Company. To them Dodge is only a county and a football team. And few of them could tell you where the towns of Chauncey and Eastman got their names.

If John Forsyth, lying in Christ Churchyard on St. Simon's Island, has been virtually forgotten along with the timber company, the same fate had not befallen the memory of Lucius Williams.

The name of Williams, chief defendant in a federal conspiracy indictment, may not be well known among the young. But it is certainly still respected among many of the older heads in these parts, even though he has been dead over a hundred years. Also still a subject of discussion is the man who was "executed" at the church on Christmas Eve Night, although he is often derisively recalled as "that man who killed my great-granddaddy."

To understand all of the ramifications of this strange affair requires an examination of the characters and family ties of the individuals concerned. The whole tragedy could be called "The Williams Connection," for Williams blood ran, both genetically and literally, through the whole affair.

All the main participants in this series of family sorrows were descendants of one couple—Joseph Williams, Jr., and his wife Mealy Bevin, both formerly of Duplin County, North Carolina. Drawn by the Georgia land lotteries, Williams, a former Lieutenant in the Revolutionary War, migrated southward about 1823. His children, mostly all married by now, came with their parents; and by the mid 1820's the various branches of his family were all firmly established in the lower part of Telfair County.

Minor supporting roles in the tragedy were played by others of the Williams clan but all the starring parts went to descendants of Joseph's daughter Elizabeth and her husband John Williams. That this couple were first cousins as was common in those days; and their offspring, with their concentrated doses of Williams' blood, staged an almost unbelievable life drama which had all the elements of a modern day soap opera. (William's parents were also first cousins.)

Although John and Elizabeth may have had more children, there is a certain record of only three. All of these children and their descendants played crucial roles in the tragedy being narrated at this time.

Emily, the oldest child of John and Elizabeth, married her first cousin Joseph B. White. It is the Whites' daughter Eliza that we need to remember.

Joseph Gooden Williams, born about 1823, was John and Elizabeth's oldest son. "Joe Good" and his wife Priscilla had, among their many children, a son named George Morris Williams. Keep an eye on that boy.

It could be truthfully stated that the leading character in the drama, which literally ripped branches from the family tree, was Lucius Williams, youngest child of John and Elizabeth. Lucius was an outstanding man in the community. A former sheriff of Telfair County, he served as a Captain in the Civil War. He was well-beloved in the community as a man who was always ready to help a neighbor, whether it was by taking in an orphan child or by constructing an expertly done coffee-pot deed, complete with government seal, for a friend who needed a quick legal paper in his fight with the Dodge Company. Lucius Williams was also a fast man with a gun and came in handy for sniping at the timber man. It could be truthfully said that all the locals considered this multi-talented gentleman to be a very valuable asset.

The federal government did not. On June 25, 1894, Norman Dodge brought a bill of peace against Lucius Williams and three hundred and eighty other persons. The suit alleged that there was a general scheme by the defendants to deprive him of his lands. Not surprisingly, the United States Court agreed with this accusation. Williams ignored all instructions of the government, perhaps even speeding up his defiance. The authorities soon found cause to call for Williams' arrest. They claimed that he had killed a Dodge Company laborer. It was an easy thing to issue a warrant for the arrest of a man like Lucius Williams. Actually finding and arresting him proved to be much more difficult.

Meanwhile, Williams' niece, Eliza White, and his nephew George Morris Williams, had been busy preparing their contributions to the coming trouble.

Eliza, at the age of twenty, had married Thomas Garrison. They had one child. And then the War came. Eliza didn't like the war. Not only had her husband joined the Confederate Armey in 1862, but other men had left as well. Scarcity of men was a major problem for Eliza. Then her eye fell on her fifteen-year-old first cousin, George Morris Williams, who proved to be a likely prospect. So in 1864, at the age of sixteen, George became the father of Eliza's son, Andrew.

Thomas Garrison returned from the war, and while it can be safely assumed that there was not joy in the old homestead when he discovered the extra child, the couple remained together. They produced other children, two of which were Bob and Cohen Garrison.

Thomas died in 1872. The child, Andrew, went at this time to live with his natural father, George Williams. Parenthetically, Eliza produced another child, Mary, two years after the death of her husband. Not much else was heard about this woman. But never mind; by producing Andrew Williams and Bob and Cohen Garrison, Eliza had made her mark on history.

George Morris Williams had, by this time, married and started a large family of legitimate children. One of his sons was Bryant Williams. We need to remember Bryant.

When, in 1854, Lucius Williams married for the first time, he had married Catherine Garrison, future sister-in-law of Eliza White. Catherine produced three children and then died during the Civil War. Her widower, in 1866, married Margaret McDermid and started a second family. When the children of Thomas Garrison were orphaned in 1872, Mr. Williams still looked on the young nephews of his first wife with kindness. (These children were also, we recall, the grandchildren of Lucius's sister, Emily Williams White.) So the Garrison children were in and out of the Williams home and it is understood that Williams contributed a great deal to their upbringing.

Whether because of their "raising" or some genetic result, the younger Garrison boys, Bob and Cohen, did not turn out as some people would have wished.

As far as the records show, they pretty much managed to stay out of trouble with the law. Nonetheless, they were both stamped with the image one might expect of a member of the James Gang. They were sharpshooters and quick to fight; a man was wise not to mess with the Garrison boys, or with their Garrison kin, for they had a great sense of family. They worked long hard hours without pay in the fields of their ailing uncle, James Garrison. And an unarmed Bob once managed, with one stroke, to disarm and disable a pistol-toting man who had dared insult this same uncle. He simply, with alarming speed, grabbed and threw a hatchet at the arm of the man drawing the gun.

As a rule, the Garrison boys got whatever they wanted, one way or another. Though not usually considered prosperous, each could appear as a well-dressed gentleman with polished manners. When Bob fell in love with raven-haired Mollie Pridgen of Coffee County, he used both charm and force to get her. He allured her with romantic letters, written "from my upstairs room where I sit dreaming of you." Actually, the letters were written from a dirt-floored cabin. Nevertheless, he won the heart of the girl.

Next came the force. Her relatives detested him. So when Bob went to marry Molly, he took reinforcements—his brother Cohen and their cohort, Lee Wells (whose grandmother was a Williams, of course). Lee and Cohen rounded up the objecting relatives and forced them at gunpoint into the family smokehouse. Before the angry family was released the next morning, Bob had got a preacher, married Molly, and spent his wedding night in the home of his incarcerated new in-laws. He then left with his bride; and neither of them ever again visited her former home.

If Bob Garrison was audacious and aggressive, his brother Cohen was more so. Although he was the younger of the two brothers, Cohen was considered the leader. Perhaps this is why the bulk of the blame for what happened has been laid at his door.

There had been prices on the heads of Lucius Williams and his sons John and Stephen (Punch) for nearly a year. John Kelly, United States Marshal, was absolutely determined to take them to Macon and thus collect the substantial reward.

But Lucius Williams knew very well every mile of swamp and woodland in the area. And with a friendly neighborhood grapevine to serve as his early warning system, he frequently knew Kelly's plans almost as soon as Kelly knew them himself. So the foxy Lucius continued to lead the frustrated Marshal a not-so-merry chase.

Once in the beginning, Williams had slipped up. Going to his hog pen deep in the woods, he laid his gun down just long enough to feed his hogs. It was too long. Soon he was handcuffed by a United States Marshal and marching toward the train station in Milan.

But the officer soon learned that even a handcuffed and disarmed Lucius Williams was a formidable foe. Using his own feet as weapons, Williams stomped the feet of his captor all the way. After they had traveled in this unpleasant fashion for a mile or so, the Marshal heard a shout. Looking around he saw a gun barrel pointing at him from behind every bush and tree. He later estimated that thirty guns had come to the aid of Williams. Soon the officer, minus his prisoner, went away cursing his luck, while a freed Lucius Williams returned to his hog pen more determined than ever to evade his would-be captors.

The prowess of Mr. Williams was a source of pride to the whole neighborhood. Man and boy alike, they all enjoyed sitting around and bragging about how "They'll never get Uncle Loosh."

During one such session, Cohen Garrison ventured another opinion. "Maybe Uncle Loosh should turn himself in. With such a big reward, somebody may kill him sooner or later."

"Naw," somebody disagreed. "They'll never get Uncle Loosh."

"Don't be too sure. I'll bet I could get him myself in a week's time," Cohen bragged.

A fellow named Little carried a report of this conversation, complete with embellishments, back to Mr. Williams, who was outraged at his audacious nephew. He sent word to Cohen to "leave the county" under threat of being killed.

But the stubborn young man wasn't budging, through his relatives spent hours trying to reason with him. "Go on," his uncle Levy Garrison advised. "In a few years you can come back, and it'll all be over."

"No, sir!" an adamant Cohen replied. "Nobody runs me off."

In a short while, Mr. Williams took a shot at Cohen from ambush. Some said that his son John deflected his father's aim. But the truth may have been that Uncle Loosh didn't really want to hit Cohen, only to scare the young whippersnapper away.

That missed shot was a big mistake. Cohen and his brother Bob promptly offered their services to United States Marshal John Kelly. But once deputized, they found that the job was not as easy nor as quick as Cohen had anticipated.

Lucius Williams and his sons continued to be elusive. Then one day, by lucky chance and diligent work, the Marshals discovered all three of them at a campsite near the Ocmulgee River. The officers had surrounded the area and were ready to move in for the capture when, to Cohen's dismay, he spotted his eighteen year old cousin Willie Garrison wandering in for a visit with the Williams men.

The planned attack was called off; and Cohen went roaring over to his Uncle Levy. "If you don't want Willie killed, you had better keep him away from Uncle Loosh. He could have had his head blown off today!"

Levy Garrison threatened his son with the ultimate skinning if he ever again went near either Lucius Williams or his cousins Bob and Cohen. But young Willie had already ruined the Marshal's present chances of getting Williams. And it was three weeks before they again saw a good chance.

The officers discovered that the Williams men had begun sneaking back to John's home every day about noon, where they enjoyed some home cooking by John's wife, Missy. Here the Marshals had them altogether. But there was a woman and children in that house, and the officers preferred trailing the men back to their campsite.

But when continued attempts to do this failed for one reason or another, Marshal Kelly lost patience and declared, "I'm not agreeable to staying down here in the woods getting chewed on by ticks all summer. We'll take them at the house at noon tomorrow."

So, on a fine day in 1895, while the Williams men ate, the three Marshals prepared themselves for the assault. Kelly mounted the roof of the house; Cohen hid in a buggy house in the front yard; and Bob positioned himself behind a fig bush in the back yard.

When Lucius Williams finished his dinner, and while the others were still inside, he took himself to the front porch for an after dinner snooze. His gun lying beside him, he had just dozed off when the action began.

The events that followed have been reported more than one way. A special news article was printed in the Macon *Telegraph* on May 21, 1895. It is reprinted below just as it appeared on that day— contents, misstated name [Luther instead of Lucius], grammatical construction and all.

LUTHER WILLIAMS KILLED

The Old Man Shot While Sleeping
On the Porch of His Son's
House

DEPUTY MARSHALLS DID IT

The Marshalls Reported to Have Kept Up
The Firing after They Had Been
Begged to Stop – A Posse
After the Officers

McRae, May 20—(Special)—A fearful homicide was committed at Cobbville, in this county, at 1 o'clock today by John Kelly, Cohen and Bob Garrison, deputy United States Marshalls.

There have been for some time criminal charges against L. L., John M. and Stephen Williams pending in federal court at Macon, growing out of the famous land trouble of this section. For a month negotiations for settlement of the Williams' have been going on, and last Friday an amicable settlement was effected through Capt. John A. Phillips, acting as the representative of Mr. Dodge. Capt. Philips met the Williams at Cobbville and a satisfactory settlement was agreed on, after which the Williams' told the Dodge people to go ahead and cut the timber on the land in dispute. They were assured by Capt. Phillips that the settlement was perfectly satisfactory and that Mr. Dodge had no desire to prosecute or molest them further, but, of course, he had no authority to settle the criminal proceedings that had grown out of the land trouble though he gave Williams every reason to believe that they would settle themselves after the prime cause of the trouble was removed. Acting on this assurance they were willing to go to Macon to answer the criminal charges against them, which were really not so serious since the charge of murder against them could not be legally sustained as they were prepared to prove an alibi, but a large reward has been offered for their arrest and Kelly, Cohen Garrison, and Bob Garrison had determined to carry them to Macon regardless of the settlement of the land troubles, and at one o'clock today they went to the residence of John M. Williams and without warning or a command to surrender they shot L.L. Williams through the head and just below the heart while he lay sleeping on the front piazza of his son's house. They riddled the house with bullets and came near killing Mrs. John L. Williams, who had just risen from a sick bed. One bullet passed through the bed and dropped onto her hand as she was about to raise her little child from the floor. She implored the officers to stop shooting as no one wanted to resist them, but they continued to riddle the house with Winchester balls, it seems, as long as there were any in their guns. John M. and Stephen Williams were arrested, handcuffed and carried away, but L.L. Williams was left for dead and will probably die.

As news of the killing spread over the country the indignation of the people increased, and at this time there is much excitement. Warrants have been sworn out against the marshals and a posse of determined men will arrest them if they can be found.

Some neighborhood accounts of what happened varied a bit from the newspaper article. According to one local version, when Mr. Williams had gotten settled down for his nap, John Kelly called down from his post on the roof, "We've got you surrounded. Come out with your hands up!"

"What's that you say?" the man on the porch shouted.

By the time Kelly had repeated his command, Lucius Williams, having located the position of the voice, had started shooting through the porch ceiling. Kelly dodged the bullets by moving farther back on the roof. When William's gun was empty, he reloaded and stepped into the yard for a better view of his target. But before he could fire, Cohen Garrison, from his vantage in the buggy house, shot his uncle Loosh.

Mr. Williams was hit, but he wasn't dead. He turned and ran for the back yard. Kelly opened up with all his fire power.

The hard hit man staggered from a wound which was to prove fatal. But he was still running. As he started for the back door of the house, Bob Garrison shot him from behind the fig tree.

The Marshals continued to fire at the house where the dying man and his two sons were hiding. When their guns were empty, and before they could reload, John's wife, Missy came out waving her apron and begging. "Please don't shoot any more. I think you've killed Mr. Williams. And the others will give up if you will stop firing."

"All right," Kelly agreed. "Go into the house and bring all the guns out. Then tell the others to come out with their hands up."

An inside-the-house version of the shooting was told later by Sally Vickery, who was ten years old as the time of the incident. Nellie's father having died, and her mother having a large number of other children, Nellie was kindly being provided for by John and Missy Williams. Much later Nellie related to her own children the story of her childhood fright and attempted escape.

According to Nellie's story, the house contained, at that time, a much larger number of people than that reported by the newspaper. There were Lucius Williams' wife Maggie, his sons Clarence and Lucius, Jr., ("Nig"), and his son-in-law Daniel Kelly, in addition to John, Punch, Missy and her child, and , of course, Nellie himself.

Missy Williams, having already caught a rifle ball in her hand, was very concerned for the safety of her baby, for it looked as if all the people in the house would surely be killed. It was decided that the only way to save the lives of the children was for Nellie to take the baby and run for a neighbor's house. Surely, the adults reasoned, the Marshals would not shoot the children.

Although the children were not shot, their escape attempt was unsuccessful, for Nellie, clutching the baby in her arms, was stopped by one of the officers and marched right back into the house from whence she came. She, too, was ordered to bring the guns into the yard and to tell the men to surrender.

Regardless of the story version, it was a fact that all the men in the house did place themselves in the custody of the United States Marshals and were soon marching toward the railroad station, leaving the dying Mr. Williams in the care of his women folks.

Children attending school on the south edge of Milan were out for afternoon recess, when a shouting man came riding hell-for-leather into town.

"They've killed Mr. Williams and taken Punch and John and all of them! Don't let them get to the train," he yelled.

So furiously had he ridden his horse, the children later recalled, that the beast fell dead from exhaustion when the ride was over.

And all to no avail. For the Marshals, expecting trouble from the local populace, had taken an indirect route to Helena, which, though a longer distance than Milan, had faster passenger service.

Once the prisoners were safely incarcerated in Macon, Cohen Garrison, sensing the mood of the community, left the county. Some said he went all the way to Mississippi.

Bob Garrison wasn't sure how bad his own position was. He correctly sensed that people blamed his brother Cohen the most. And knowing his own skill with a gun, he decided to stay where he was. But he was never without that gun, sleeping with it under his pillow. His instincts proved right, for several years passed, and no one tried to harm him.

Lucius Williams lies buried in the Blockhouse Churchyard on Georgia Highway 117 just outside Jacksonville, Ga. Blockhouse had been the site of church worship since the early days when it had been a blockhouse or fort for protection from the Indians. And within a few years of the burial of Lucius Williams, it became the scene of a bizarre continuation of the war that took his life.

During Cohen Garrison's "sojourn in a foreign land" he had married and fathered a child. When his wife died and he was given the sole responsibility of a small daughter, he began to re-think his reason for exile. Eight years had passed. Surely by now, he decided, the community's anger had subsided. So taking his child, he turned his face toward home.

He had not been back in Telfair County very long before a meeting was called. Most of the Williams men were there, plus several of their friends and relatives. The question was not whether Cohen Garrison would be killed. That was a foregone conclusion. This assembly was for the purpose of deciding who would do the job.

Years later, when he was an old man, Tal Wells confided to a friend that he had been present at that meeting. Thanks to his paternal grandmother, Williams blood flowed in the Wells veins, and he had readily agreed to hold the straws as the Williams men lined up for a chance at the short straw and the job of getting Cohen Garrison.

The "lucky" man was Tripp Williams, according to Well's story. Tripp was the grandson of Lucius Williams by his first wife Catherine Garrison. Thus he was also the first cousin of the man he had been selected to kill.

Being part of an assembly proposing such as a bold step as a revenge killing must had been heady stuff to young Tripp. And now he had a chance to be the hero, the avenger of the Williams clan. He looked at the short straw he held in fingers.

Then the enormity and finality of the step he was about to take started to creep into his thinking. Reality was hard to face. He could, by killing his cousin, earn the admiration of his fellow conspirators. But he would also forever merit his own self-condemnation as a killer. That he could not face; and he flung the straw from his hand. "I won't do it! Not kill him!" he declared.

Silence prevailed for the space of a minute. Then, slowly, Bryant Williams stepped forward. Bryant was, we remember, a legitimate son of George Morris Williams, and therefore half brother to Andrew Williams, who was himself half brother of the intended victim. Bryant held his own straw up for all to see.

21

"By my calculations," he declared. "This straw right here is the next shortest one. I'll volunteer for the job."

Bryant Williams had contracted for a difficult undertaking. He was aware of Cohen Garrison's expertise with a gun. And he knew that if he were not careful, he would end up being the corpse himself. The key to the success of his job, as he saw it, was to shoot Cohen at a time and place where the victim would not get a chance to shoot first. After much careful thought Bryant came up with a brilliant plan for creating that ideal condition.

It was Christmas Eve Night in the year of 1903. The neighborhood was gathered for services in Blockhouse Church. Cohen Garrison was there, too, along with his small daughter. Beside them sat Leila Williams, five year old daughter of Andrew Williams, Cohen's half brother. After the service, Cohen picked up his child, and with his niece Leila and several other little girls trailing along, he made for the church door. Once he reached the top doorstep, he put down his daughter in order to have both hands free to light his pipe.

One shot rang out and he fell dead amidst a horrified group of children.

Andrew Williams was there in the church that evening. This son of George Williams and Eliza Garrison loved all his brothers. He had no idea of the plans his relatives had for Cohen. But after seeing his maternal half brother fall, he quickly learned what was soon to be an open neighborhood secret—that the killer was his own father's son, Bryant Williams.

But Andrew knew nothing constructive that he could do with that knowledge. He could only reach down and take his newly-orphaned niece into his arms.

Whether because even his own co-conspirators may have been unhappy with his selecting the church premises for an execution site or whether he feared the arm of the law, Bryant Williams quickly left to spend the rest of his life in Florida.

Bob Garrison left too, to step quickly into another unusual adventure.

Thus, with Cohen Garrison buried in an unmarked grave only a few yards from the tomb of his Uncle Loosh, all the principals of this affair were gone from the local scene. But they had created a legend which lives on until this day.

The Garrison-McMillan Alliance

Bob Garrison and his family packed for a move the day after his brother Cohen was killed. He did not feel the need to go far, however. For in those days, if one left the county, he was not likely to be followed.

In Dodge County there were natural mineral springs located at a place called Jaybird. The springs were owned by Tom McMillan and had become a favored recreational site.

However, Mr. McMillan, who did not live on this particular property, had a very big problem, a problem named Anderson.

Anderson was a much-feared bully who had without any right or legal maneuver, simply moved to Jaybird Springs and taken it for his own. Mr. McMillan tried legal action, but it didn't work. The law officers were afraid to evict Anderson.

Bob Garrison needed a new home; Mr. McMillan needed to recover his property. They decided that perhaps both of their problems could have the same solution. Mr. McMillan offered Bob Garrison a free ten year lease on the facilities in return for Garrison freeing the place of Anderson.

Bob Garrison did not propose to use his gun to rid the place of its human pest, even though his reputation as a skillful gun slinger had reached into Dodge County. However, when Bob moved into the area, Anderson, having heard these reports, knew that he was not facing an easily frightened man.

So Anderson watched as Garrison constructed facilities on the opposite side of the springs. Soon the bully realized that he had unbeatable competition, for Bob Garrison, bankrolled by McMillan, was offering free swimming and free drinks to his customers.

Anderson, having no customers, soon packed up and left. McMillan once more had control of his property. The Garrisons had made a home and a lifetime friend. They lived at Jaybird Springs for many years, and most of them are buried in a small private cemetery along with the McMillans.

Old Sins and Long Shadows

One of Cohen Garrison's cousins was once heard to remark that Bob and Cohen were too mean to be Garrisons. "Their pa was undoubtedly a stray Yankee soldier," he declared. That this wasn't true was evidenced by the fact that a Garrison family resemblance once landed in peril a cousin who was born five years after the death of Cohen. Since Cohen had been dead for more than forty years when the incident occurred, this younger relative concluded that old sins really do have long shadows.

Saxton Garrison, son of Cohen's first cousin Levy, often went to Coffee County to buy tobacco plants for his farm. It was on such an occasion that Saxton found himself in danger.

As he and his farm hands pulled and packed the plants, he noticed an old man sitting on a nearby log. Saxton felt the eyes of the old man following him. So he wasn't surprised when the man approached to question, "Who are you?"

"I'm Saxton Garrison."

"Where are you from?"

"Telfair County."

Then to the amazement of all those around, the aged gentlemen grabbed a limb and went on the attack. It turned out that this old man was one of the brothers whom Cohen had imprisoned in the smokehouse on the occasion of the Bob Garrison—Molly Pridgen wedding.

Saxton Garrison then fully believed that his own father was quite correct when he often said "Boy, you're the spitting image of my late Cousin Cohen!"

Beware!

Andrew Garrison was a very dangerous man—or so he said.

Actually, those who knew him were convinced that he would never hurt a soul. In fact, one had trouble recollecting occasions on which he had even engaged in a verbal battle.

This youngest son of James and Nancy Jane Rawlins Garrison had grown up in the shadow of daring men. His parents had both died by the time he was eight; and a teenage brother became guardian of his younger siblings. The reckless Bob and Cohen Garrison frequently looked in on their first cousins. And Andrew listened with admiration to the tales of their escapades.

Perhaps he was not made of brave material. Or perhaps it was caused from his position as low man on the totem pole during his growing up years. But for whatever reason, Andrew never had the courage to commit the deeds of derring-do which he so much admired in others.

Except in his dreams—which he frequently translated into fearsome tales. For Andrew, whose prematurely white hair and large blue eyes gave him the appearance of a well-worn angel, liked to share his raw courage recklessness with all who would listen.

All his violent behavior always took place outside the county. Once off his home ground, Andrew and his .38 did terrible things. Like the time over in Abbeville, when he shot a man or two and frightened everybody out of the saloon.

If no one ever remembered Andrew in a hostile mood; no one ever saw his .38, either.

Perhaps, he thought that if he showed it, someone might counter it with a .45.

As it was, there was no danger. Even though, when it came to tales of courage and naked belligerence, the gentle Andrew Garrison was a very fast draw.

To Shoot a Gun and Not His Mouth

In the spring of 1862, the three older brothers of Levy Garrison (the first one) had gone away to war. The oldest brother had died soon afterwards. However, this event did not deter young Levy's enthusiasm for "joining up".

His mother, Sarah, felt differently. She brought up every reason she could think of in an effort to dissuade him from joining the Confederate Army. Finally, in desperation, she said, "Levy, you can't go to war; you can't even talk."

To which, Levy, who had severe speech impediment, replied undauntedly, "Th-th-that's all-ll r-right, M-M-Ma. Th- They d-don't w-want m-me t' t-t-talk. Th-they w-w-want m-me to sh-sh-shoot."

The Old Soldier

Duncan Cameron, who was, because of his small stature, called Short Duncan, was well known as a Telfair County wit. He claimed that during the war, a Yankee bullet had dented his skull. And, according to Duncan, all that the doctor did was to pull on a corkscrew which he had inserted into the depression; and the skull popped back into place, just as if the dent had been in a tin bucket.

He never tired of telling about his escapades during the war. So, when in the early 1920's, it was announced that an old soldiers reunion was to be held in Texas, it was not surprising that Duncan Cameron was right ready to load up and go.

Telfair County's old veterans chose to ride in Texas on the train, which was, in those days, a very popular means of transportation.

However, a popular place is often a crowded place. So it was with the train on which Short Duncan traveled. It was so full that, when the train stopped somewhere near the Alabama-Mississippi border, there were no more available seats. And a pretty girl about eighteen years old was forced to stand.

Mr. Cameron looked at her and said teasingly, "Honey, there's no call for you to stand up. Why don't you sit right here on my knee. I'm an old man. It'll be all right."

Perhaps to the old soldier's surprise, the girl accepted his invitation and plopped herself down on his knee.

They had ridden only a few miles in this position, when Mr. Cameron suddenly tapped the girl's shoulder and said, "Honey, I think you had better get up. I'm not as old as I thought I was!"

Court is in Session
(Or is it a Circus?)

The rambunctious character of the people of early Telfair County was nowhere better reflected than in their Superior Court minutes.

The earliest Telfair County court met 16th April 1810 in the home of John Peterson. John's fellow citizens rewarded their host's hospitality by indicting him for assault and battery.

This precedent was faithfully followed in 1811 when court convened in the home of Mark Pridgen. Mr. Pridgen was indicted, and eventually convicted, of adultery and retailing spirituous liquors without a license.

Mr. Pridgen's legal problems continued in 1813, when the court was required to arbitrate a property dispute between Mark and his wife, Sarah.

The couple brought their problems before the court for a third time, when in 1816, she sued for divorce. In spite of Mr. Pridgen's earlier conviction for adultery, his wife was refused a divorce and was forced by the court to pay the cost of the trial.

None the less, Sarah Pridgen had the last laugh. Her unwanted husband, Mark, mysteriously disappeared. It was rumored that he met an untimely end at the hands of Indians. But some people, having reflected on the nature of his marital life, have wondered about other possible explanations for his disappearance.

When, in 1819, Abraham Powell, another prominent Telfair Countian, left the local scene, nobody wondered where he had gone. Everyone knew that he had gone to the state prison for perjury.

Early court records were peppered with the name of Abraham Powell; He was both a member of the jury and under indictment, sometimes at the same time. In October of 1815, Mr. Powell was foreman of the grand jury, stepping down from his leadership position only temporarily while his fellow jurors returned a true bill for assault and battery against their foreman.

It is also in 1815 records, buried in Telfair County Deed Book D, pages 123-126, that one can find accounts of other acts and quarrels involving Mr. Powell. Here, Mr. Thomas Swain published a very harsh rebuke against the character of Mr. Powell, who at the time was running for State Senator from Telfair. Mr. Swain accuses the candidate of libel, being a false witness, stealing the neighbors' timber, and manipulating the Telfair County tax collection for his own benefit. Mr. Swain's accusation ends with the hope that Abraham Powell's "future course of life may be so...that he will not call upon myself or the public again to take any further notice of him."

According to the record, quite a bit of notice had already been taken of Mr. Powell by Doctor Thomas Moore, who had threatened to give Powell a beating for publicly calling Dr. Moore "a federalist".

This threat was apparently heeded by Powell, who decided to recant. Thomas Swain, obviously not a fan of Powell's, maintained that Abraham Powell's subsequent signed statement retracting his accusations against Moore was because of "his dastardly fear of being caned." That might well have been true, for Abraham Powell, standing only 5 feet, 4 ¾ inches tall, could have been an easy man to whip. (See *Georgia Black Book: Morbid, Macabre, and Sometimes Disgusting Records of Genealogical Value* by Robert Scott Davis, Jr.)

To give more justification to the reasonableness of Powell's "dastardly fear," the author notes that whipping somebody was one of the more frequently indicted offenses in early Telfair Courts. There were also variations on this offense as is shown by the indictment against James Rouse and William Willis for "maiming".

Thomas Pridgen, Thomas Aultman, William Wilson, Washington Irving, Charles Booker, and William McCrimmon were among those who sometimes preferred their violence on a grander scale than a mere "whipping". They were all, at one time or another, indicted for rioting.

In 1834, the ultimate in violence was brought before the Telfair County Court. William Parker and Lazarus Williams were accused of the murder of Hugh Cook. They were shipped off to the Pulaski County jail because that of Telfair was "unsafe".

A son of George Cook and Jane Ashley, Hugh was a former sheriff of Telfair County and in 1829 was serving as the local prosecutor, during which time he was indicted for malpractice in office. Cook was married to Milsey Mariah, William Parker's only daughter.

Unfortunately, the Superior Court minutes do not contain any material regarding a possible motive for the crime. Little is known of the character of the man who was supposedly killed by his father-in-law. Was he a wife- beater? Was he a quarrelsome man who was loathed by the community at large?

Or was his father-in-law an undesirable man given to violence?

The jury thought not. William Parker was acquitted.

But whether his acquittal came at the hands of "twelve good men and true" was open to question, for shortly afterwards, one of the jurors, Mark Wilcox, was indicted for perjury involving his conduct during the trial. Wilcox is described in the indictment as "not having the fear of God before his eyes nor regarding the law of this state, but being moved and seduced by the instigation of the devil and contriving and intending to prevent the due course of the law." The grand jury alleged that Mr. Wilcox "falsely swore that he had not already formed and expressed an opinion as to the guilt" of William Parker.

In spite of such a stinging indictment, the petit jury chose to acquit Mark Wilcox.

Perhaps Lazarus Williams, the other man accused of the murder of Hugh Cook, came out of the affair even better. This researcher can find no record of Mr. Williams ever being brought to trial for this crime.

Just as the record gives no theory of motive for the killing, it does not show a connection between the two men jointly accused of the murder. However, Lazarus Williams and William Parker's wife were first cousins. And William Parker was probably the uncle of Lazarus's wife. In addition, tradition states that Lazarus Williams was William Parker's overseer.

However vaguely they address the rest of the case, the records do at least hint at the means by which Williams managed to avoid trial and conviction. It appears that the prosecutor's case rested on the testimony of two witnesses, James Wall and Mary Roberts. These Witnesses had vacated the county. And no amount of threats of legal action served to bring them to testify. This convenient unavailability, along with the sheriff's negligence in failing to send out notices to the jurors for one session of court, kept delaying the murder trial.

Meanwhile Lazarus Williams loudly demanded a speedy trial, knowing well that, without its star witnesses, the state had no case.

By 1839, Williams, having apparently beaten the murder indictment, had moved to Irwin County and gotten himself indicted for gambling.

John Grimes was another illegal gambler. In 1856, this high roller was indicted in Telfair County for "playing cards with a Negro for the purpose of winning a drink of liquor."

However, gambling does not appear to have been considered a grievous crime, as indictments for this vice were infrequent. Adultery, on the other hand, was often the basis of court disputes. Among those early Telfair Countians stamped with the scarlet letter were Arch McDuffie, Rhoda Brantley, Mary Martin, Wiley Howard, Polly Winslow, Jincey Ford, and William Studstill.

In time, the Telfair Court quit featuring adultery cases, but it never ceased to be colorful. Just after the turn of this century, much flamboyance was added to the local courtroom by Lovett Harrell, Attorney-at-Law.

On one occasion the opposing attorney objected to Mr. Harrell's abusive cross-examination of a witness. The judge sustained the objection, adding "Mr. Harrell, you must stop maligning Mrs. Burkhalter's character!"

"I am sorry," Mr. Harrell replied." I didn't at all mean to throw off on her character. But the truth is, Your Honor, I didn't know that Mrs. Burkhalter had a character."

Lovett Harrell was known for his ability to get his own way in spite of rulings from the bench. Having the philosophy that the older a case is, the weaker it is, this attorney always endeavored to postpone trial for his client.

It seemed on one occasion that his luck had run out. In spite of Harrell's pleas that his chief witness was out of state, the judge was insistent that the case be tried "this very day."

"All right, Your Honor," Mr. Harrell seemed to agree, "I'll go on without my witness, but could I please have until after lunch to reorganize my defense?"

"Very well," the judge replied. "You may have that much time, but not a minute longer."

After the noon recess, the attorneys took their places and court convened. As Mr. Harrell rose to his feet to begin his opening remarks, he seemed to stagger. He clutched his chest and fell to the floor in obvious pain.

So Lovett Harrell's case was continued until the next term of court, for, as the judge was forced to concede, the defense attorney, a very necessary instrument of justice, was too ill to proceed with his role.

School—and Prayer

Alaben School, named for a popular Methodist minister, was located on what is now known as Milan Cemetery Road. The majority of the students were Cravey descendants.

As Saxton Garrison reported:

The school was about a mile north of our house. The road we walked went through the woods, where there were several useful fallen logs. My sister, Eva, took advantage of one of them, in the case of the despised petticoat that Ma made her wear to school. As we got beyond the sight of home, Eva peeled off that petticoat, stuffed it in a hollow log, and then donned it again on the way home from school. These steps were taken many times, for Ma insisted on that petticoat quite often.

When my ugly brown coat problem arose on the first frosty morning of the season, I could envision being plagued by that coat for many winters to come. It looked almost impossible to ever outgrow a coat that big and baggy. Ma had made me put on that coat, which I was sure had won a national ugly coat award. Something had to be done lest I had to hunt me a hollow log every chilly morning. I needed a permanent solution.

That first morning, after I had put it on, I ran all the way to school in order to get there early. I took off the coat and stuffed it in the back of a desk.

As the schoolroom started to fill up, one of the other boys spied a coat sleeve that I had left hanging out.

"Whose coat is this?" was the question that went all around the room.

Everybody denied ownership. I was among them; and neither Eva nor my brother Morgan told on me.

Soon someone (I admit I was the one.) suggested that we play tug-of-war with the coat at recess. Afterwards I threw the remains into the bushes to wait for me until school let out.

When I wore what little was left of that ugly thing into the house, Ma spied the tatters and demanded, "Who tore up this coat?"

"Some of the boys at school," I replied, neglecting to let it be known that I was front and center of the destruction.

I was real proud to think that no one would ever wear that ugly coat again.

The coat was not the only thing that got shredded at school. One of the Knight boys always stayed on the front page of his reader. It was not that he was too dumb to learn to read. It was just that as soon as he mastered a page, he ate it. There sat John Knight chewing the paper much like a cow chewed her cud.

More memorable than John's page eating was the event that happened on April 1. Miss Tealie Seigler was firm in her intention to punish the boys for that outrage.

It had all started as an innocent April Fool's Day joke. A before-school student conference had decided that it would be a great prank if all Miss Seigler's pupils disappeared from school. It was to be done in shifts. The boys would all skip out before the take-in bell rang. During the morning recess, they would be joined by the girls, who would bring the lunches, which were now all stacked on a table in the school's one classroom.

But as that morning wore on, several of the leaders among the girls became doubters; and by recess time, the great April Fools Day joke had lost its female component entirely.

At first the boys thought that the girls were just late. But by lunchtime, their growling stomachs declared that the joke was on them, for in this case, AWOL meant absent without lunch.

The boys had discovered that even a good joke has its price. And the price of this one was too high, so they sneaked back to school, intent on digging into their lunch buckets.

Miss Tealie had different plans. She had suggested that the girls eat lunch inside that day. A nice little hen party they would have, and no boys allowed. She refused to let the runaways back inside the schoolroom.

The hungry boys couldn't figure a way to get their lunches, until they looked up the road and saw Aunt Becky and Uncle John coming by the schoolhouse in their buggy. John and Becky Cravey were parents of Loch and Gus, two of the boys involved, as well as being related, in one way or another, to nearly all the others. Surely they would help, the boys reasoned. It was to Aunt Becky, who was known to be a softy, that the hungry boys poured out their sad story.

And just as they had suspected she would do, Aunt Becky marched right into that schoolhouse and confronted Miss Tealie for "treating these poor little young'uns this-a-way."

"But, Mrs. Cravey," the teacher replied. "I can't let them get by with this. You do know that. Exactly what would you do if you were in my place?"

"Well, let me see. I believe I would—," said Aunt Becky, pausing to think. "I'd—I know just the thing for you to do, Miss Tealie. Why don't we kneel down and pray with these boys?"

And so it was decided. Soon all the males, plus Miss Tealie and Aunt Becky, were kneeling in a circle. Starting with Eschol Cravey, they began to pray. Dan Williams, Jim Knight, Gus Cravey, Saxton Garrison, each boy prayed in his turn. Until it became Loch Cravey's turn. He absolutely refused to pray.

But the real trouble came from Gus. Upon hearing his brother Loch refused to pray, Gus went immediately into a rage. His problem was not so much that his brother wouldn't pray, but that Gus himself had already prayed and couldn't "take it back".

Modifying the Car

Gus Cravey need not have fretted overly much about his regretted prayer, for it certainly had done little to change his basic nature. He was as sharp as ever in organizing and executing mischief.

As Saxton Garrison recalled:

It was about two weeks after the prayers on April 1, when a car was completely changed as it sat just down the road from the school.

There was a fella named Martin who ran a sawmill over on the Jim Vaughn place. He had a car back in the days when hardly anybody but doctors had cars.

He was on his way to Milan to catch the train to Savannah when, about a quarter of a mile below the school, his car quit on him. He knew that if he took time to work on it, he would miss his train. So he walked on into town, planning on seeing about the car after his return trip.

When we got out for the first recess, we boys ran down to inspect that car. Gus said, "Now we don't know exactly what all it's gonna take. So tomorrow bring all the tools you can".

I like to think that, if I had been a little older, I would have known better. But at the time, my mind was set on following the big boys. So I swiped some of Pa's tools. Luckily we were having a late cold snap. So I was able to wear a coat to help hide those tools.

At recess, the girls were playing hopscotch or doing whatever else they did. Miss Tealie was in the schoolhouse. After Aunt Becky's prayer meeting, she probably didn't want to see any boys. So, undisturbed, we boys fell in on that car.

There were Gus and Loch Cravey, Bart and Gert Smith, John and Jim Knight, and some others. My brother, Morgan, was home sick, so he wasn't into it.

We worked fast, and stripped that car down to where there wasn't anything left but the body and the block.

I wanted some of the little steel balls to shoot marbles. But the big boys got those. They also got the wheels, which would have been fun to roll around. In fact, they got all the things that I would have had any use for.

But since everyone else was getting some of the car parts, I wanted something, too. I was disappointed that the only thing they left for me was a piston and connecting rod. I didn't have any idea what it was, or what use I could make of it. In the spirit of one who wanted to be one of the boys, I took it anyway.

But I had too much sense to be seen with it at home. If Pa happened to spy it, I had a good notion of what he would do. Then a good idea came to me.

A flower pit that was being built for Ma. Its double brick walls had sawdust between them for insulation. When I was sure no one was looking, I shoved my contraband booty way down between those walls and made sure it was well covered with sawdust.

When word got out about what had happened to Martin's car, folks laid it to John Knight and Gus and Loch Cravey. No one mentioned me in connection with it. And I wasn't about to tell on myself.

Friends

There was a man named Studstill in the Telfair County Jail awaiting trial for murder. That presented a problem for Francis McEachin, because Studstill was a son-in-law of John Morrison Cravey, a close friend of Mr. McEachin.

There were other men who were also offended by Studstill's incarceration. So a group of the prisoner's supporters paid a call to the sheriff. It was a friendly visit. But at some point during all the swapping of tales, the joking, and the laughing, one of the companionable visitors swiped the jailhouse keys.

Then later, under cover of darkness, someone unlocked the cell door; and the prisoner went free. Yet everyone in on the conspiracy knew that freedom would be short-lived if the defendant were not removed from the area.

Francis McEachin organized a plan to get the freed man to the McEachin farm. There he provided two fast horses, one for Studstill, and another for a guide who knew the best route of escape.

Afterwards, when the defendant was adequately removed from the reach of the long arm of the law, Mr. McEachin assured his friend John Morrison Cravey, "He's safe. And don't even think of paying me anything. I don't charge you a cent for what I did. After all, that's what friends are for."

Young Bud Knowles also thought that friends deserved special attention, although of a different kind than that given by Mr. McEachin.

At Alaben School, there was, of course, no water fountain. Student thirst was quenched by having a big bucket of water, along with a common dipper, passed down the schoolroom aisles. (Note: There is a statute of limitations on penalty for such unsanitary practices.)

On the day when Bud Knowles was assigned to pass the water around, he went right on by Sidney Howard, the new boy in school.

Sidney, who was not at all popular, partly because he was considered the teacher's pet, complained, "Miss Tealie, Bud didn't let me have any water".

"Bud Knowles! You know better than that. Give Sidney some water!" She ordered.

"Don't worry, Miss Tealie", Bud replied. "I'll give him some. I just want to pass it to my friends first".

The Train Robber

Saxton Garrison would not have called himself Sidney Howard's friend. But, for more than one reason, he did go over to play at Sidney's house a good bit.

The family was interesting. Mr. and Mrs. Howard, along with their only child, had moved onto a farm adjoining that of the Garrisons. They came from Indiana or Illinois, or one of those far-off places. Saxton wasn't sure, for the parents, nor Sidney, talked about their past.

The Howards had nice furniture, and lots of books. And quite fascinating to Saxton, who was used to drawing water from a well by means of a bucket and tackle, Mr. Howard had rigged up a series of cups in a chain. One had only to stand in the kitchen, turn a crank and the cups full of water came right into the house!

Yet, if the truth be told, all this may not have provided enough attraction to pull Saxton over to the Howard Place. The real magnet was Sidney's pony and cart. That fact drove Saxton to spend quite a bit of time with Sidney.

Sidney's parents didn't seem to pay attention much to a visiting neighbor young'un. But Saxton watched them a lot.

He began to notice that Mr. Howard took fairly frequent trips, staying gone for two or more weeks at a time. He could tell when the man was due back home, because Mrs. Howard would begin pacing back and forth in front of the house.

When she heard horses' hooves sound on the wooden bridge that crossed the branch, she ran out to meet her husband. As she held out her apron, he filled it full of gold coins from the sack he held.

Saxton came to the conclusion that Mr. Howard was a train robber. Was this opinion only the fruit of a boy's active imagination?

Then the Howards suddenly sold their farm and household goods, and moved off to who knew where. Levy Garrison helped haul away much of the newly sold goods. That's when word got out that some of Mr. Howard's extensive library consisted of law books.

Throughout the rest of his childhood, Saxton kept his thoughts on the Howards to himself, never telling an adult about his train robber ideas.

The Cart Ride

Sidney Howard was gone off somewhere, but he had left half of his main attraction behind. As Saxton recalled:

Pa bought the pony cart for us young'uns. But he said the pony was only a useless animal to feed. So we made our own arrangements about getting the cart pulled.

Sister Eva, Brother Morgan, a little black girl named Gussie, and I planned on that cart taking us to the other side of a pine thicket where we would have a picnic. One of us would be the pony. However, there was not easy agreement on who would get that job. Morgan and I both wanted to be the pony. He was three years older than I, and intended to get his way. So after a little argument, I gave in, and he became the designated pony.

We put Morgan, the pony, in a pen, and fed and watered him. Then the rest of us prepared a picnic lunch.

We peeled back the bark on a fallen dead tree and caught the wood lice, which we thought would make good fried chicken. And we made mud pies. To tell the truth, I didn't ever care much for them. But Gussie was right partial to them.

Before we got the lunch packed into the cart, Morgan was stomping, pawing, and snorting in his pen. We soon stopped that by hitching him to the cart. There was a right sharp discussion about who would be the driver. I thought it should be me, because I was a boy. But Eva pulled rank, declaring that the oldest should drive. I let her have her way, but I was a little peeved. While she got herself a driving switch, I was praying that God would do a miracle and suddenly change me into the oldest child.

After we got loaded into the cart, Eva gave Morgan a good whack with her switch that made him start off right fast.

The path through the pines went down a fairly steep hill. Our pony was going faster than any of us wanted. The truth was that he was not pulling the cart; it was pushing him. Faster and faster and faster!

Then he ran over a tree root and our pony completely lost control He ran into a tree; the cart turned over, and poured us all out.

We weren't really hurt, except for a little skinned place on Gussie's knee. The only other result of the cart wreck was that Morgan's mind was changed. He never wanted to be a pony again.

I declare. Young'uns don't have fun like they used to.

Spells and Witches

To put it mildly, Pugh Francis Asbury Richard Thomas Webb was superstitious, While it was common in the earlier days for one to have at least a light coating of the stuff, Mr. Webb had been immersed in the barrel of superstition above his "head, neck, and ears" and left to soak for a very long time. And his neighbors, both black and white, took advantage of this fact.

Once, Mr. Webb had ridden into town, sporting a fine horse and brand-new, fancy saddle. On his way home, a rainstorm overtook him; and he quickly rode his steed into a neighboring barn. Here he left the horse, while he himself went into the farmhouse to wait out the duration of the storm in the company of his host.

A group of neighborhood boys had also taken shelter in the barn, admiring that new saddle. Knowing well the weakness of Mr. Webb, they came up with a devilish plan.

Without going out into the weather, they were well able to gather enough materials to enable them to go to work on their plan. A hank of horse hair from the mare in the back stall, a piece of twine, handful of hay, and a corn shuck or two and they were ready to go to work.

After the rain had slacked, and he had returned to the barn to collect his mount, Mr. Webb was horrified at the condition of his saddle, which was ornamented with tassels of this and streamers of that.

It was clear to him that, whilst he chatted in the farmhouse, some witch had put a spell on his saddle. And he had absolutely no use for bewitched possessions. Looking around, he found a longer than ten foot pole, which he used to try to push the saddle off the horse's back.

One of the watching boys asked, "Mr. Webb, would you like for us to take the saddle off for you?"

He would. And they did, leaving him to vacate the premises riding bareback. Soon Mr. Webb's ex-saddle could be observed between another horse and the behind of a certain laughing boy.

But not even that boy could beat Will Cray at relieving Webb of his possessions.

One year, the Webbs had made a bumper crop of very fine sweet potatoes, which were then safely stored for the winter in wigwam-like "banks" made of pine straw and layers of dirt.

Will Cray loved sweet potatoes. But he didn't have any of his own; and money was short. The more he thought about Mr. Webb's sweet potatoes waiting in those banks, the more his mouth watered.

If Will Cray was short of potatoes and money, he was long on resourcefulness.

One frosty morning, Mr. Webb went out to get sweet potatoes for his wife to bake for dinner. Pulling back their cover of straw, he reached for a potato. His hand closed instead around a ball of beeswax and horsehair. He flung the horror from him!

About that time, Will Cray, who had been watching from a distance, came forward to sympathize with Webb in his time of trouble.

"What will I do, Will?" Mr. Webb moaned. "I've found a witch's ball in my potato bank.

"That's bad. That's sure enough bad."

"I know that! Terrible things happen to people when a spell has been put on them. What I need to know is what I can do about it."

"That's easy. You've got to find somebody to rub out that spell."

"But who?"

"Well, Mr. Webb," said Cray, pulling himself to a greater height, "I don't like to brag, but I've got a right smart of experience doing that myself."

"You have?" the frightened Webb asked hopefully.

"But some spells is real bad to get off you."

Mr. Webb's face fell.

"Yes, sir, this looks like a real bad one. Right powerful."

Webb looked ready to cry.

"Putting my mind to it real hard, I can't think of but one thing that will work," continued Will.

"What's that?"

"These here 'taters, every last one of them has got to be hauled off. Got plumb away from here."

"You sure that will work?"

"I believe so. I recollect my daddy telling about a similar case at one time. Getting rid of them 'witched 'taters is the onliest thing that will do the trick."

"But who can I get to haul them off for me?"

"Well, it sure won't do to ask just anybody. The thing's got to be done right or it won't work. But I tell you what I'll do. I reckon you could talk me into getting rid of them for you. And seeing that you always been a good neighbor to me, I'll do it free of charge."

So Pugh Francis Asbury Richard Thomas Webb spent a season safe from the spell placed in his potato bank. And Will Cray's whole bunch seemed a little fatter than usual that winter.

Second Sight

"Second sight," sometimes called "the sight," is an ability to see things beyond the dimension in which humans live and function. These may be things in the future, or that are in the past or present, but are beyond the ability of the ordinary person to perceive.

This sight is not something one is taught like the skill to "talk out the fire" from victims of burns. It is simply an ability that one has or he doesn't. It is said that people of Celtic ancestry like the Scots or Irish are more likely to possess this sight.

Catherine (Katie) Harrell Rawlins was one who had both Irish genes and the second sight. Not all such sight is manifest in the same way. It is almost as if each individual with the sight is a specialist. Katie

Rawlins' specialty was seeing a relative in living flesh shortly after the person had died. When the steamboat, the *General Manning*, exploded on the Ocmulgee River, she saw her brother, John Harrell, who was one of those killed in the accident.

In 1981, "Grandma Katie," as she was known by her many descendants, lost her thirteen- year-old grandson, John Garrison. About the time of his death from typhoid fever, she saw him astride a horse, with a white dove riding beside him on the saddle.

Katie Rawlins died at the age of 89, having outlived half of her twelve children. In 1893, she and her granddaughter, Angela Studstill, were out in the woods, picking up "fat lightered," which is pine wood so permeated with resin that it readily burns, making it useful to start fires. Mrs. Rawlins looked up and saw her son, Redding, walking toward them.

She turned to her granddaughter. "Angela, drop the wood out of your apron. I see Redding coming, and he gets angry at the thought of his mother gathering wood. We'll pick our splinters back up when he leaves."

She started walking to meet her son. But he was no longer there. Redding Rawlins had just died.

Some people consider second sight a rare and desirable gift. Others think it reeks of witchcraft. Dyal Garrison, one of Grandma Katie's great-grandsons, seemed to be of the latter persuasion.

In 1936, Dyal had married Cassie Chambers, and moved with his beloved, brown-eyed bride into a farmhouse near Midway Methodist Church.

Late one afternoon, Dyal got a bucket and went out to the barn to milk his cow. Scarcely had streams of milk hit the bottom of the milk bucket before a voice asked, "Boy, what are you doing?"

Dyal looked up and saw his father standing there. He flung down the bucket and fled the barn. The problem was that his father, Mark, had been dead for two years.

Dyal ran into the farmhouse and after a few hurried words with his wife, they began packing all their household goods. By daybreak, they were moving all their gear into another house. (The cow and milk bucket went along as well.)

What some would have considered a wonderful chance to chat with a good, but deceased, father, scared the wax out of Dyal. He seemed to see such an opportunity as totally incompatible with the core of his being.

Dyal was not usually a person to fling things down and run. It has been suggested that the night he fled was the only time he ever got in a hurry. He was easy-going, soft-spoken, and peaceful. He and Cassie lived long and happily, raising five outstanding children. They were always friendly and hospitable. It was a delight to see them together, for as long as they both were alive, they held hands wherever they went.

Dyal's mother died in 1961, having out-lived her husband twenty-seven years. A sad-feeling Dyal was out in the field one day soon after his mother's death. She appeared to him, saying, "Don't worry about me. I'm all right."

According to one of his children, Dyal took great comfort in her words. What was the difference between her visit and that of his father many years before?

However it may seem on the surface, the circumstantial evidence suggests that the two visions seemed different to Dyal. No one knows that he put it into so many words, but he appeared to view one as "blessed assurance" and the other as well... something he instinctively knew he didn't need, an offering he was unwilling to accept.

The way Dyal reacted to the "vision" in his barn, as well as the way he lived his life, suggests that he already had the only "gift" he wanted. He had Cassie.

John Feltson Parker (Uncle Felts)

Doing Their Own Thing

The children of Samuel and Alice Parker might well be called nineteenth century hippies for they certainly did not follow the social guidelines set up for the day. Nancy Jane and Polly Ann (Pop), the two older girls, had neither chick nor husband, but children they did have, several each. Neither did Letha, called Puss, nor her brother Feltson ever marry. But as far as is known, they did not have children. Perhaps they could not have done their own thing as well had they been tied down with children.

None of these siblings were lazy good-for-nothings. The girls were considered expert weavers, and Felts employed himself as a farm hand. But when farm life got too dull for him here, he loaded his sister Puss and all their essentials into a one horse wagon and took off for Pensacola, Florida. The trip usually lasted about two years during which time the two tried their hands at Florida farming.

With this wandering in his blood, we know that Felts Parker was not a draft dodger because he was a home body. Nor was it because of religious scruples, for he was not a noticeably devout man. Felts hid out during the Civil War for one reason—pure cowardice. A small man, who was not even given to facing an unarmed enemy, he certainly had no stomach for facing a Yankee gun. When someone teased that he could have been a war hero, he said, "No, I would have been dead."

Aunt Puss, as she was known to the neighborhood children, had quite a reputation as a story teller. The more gruesome the story, the more likely that it was in Aunt Puss' repertoire. Ghosts and goblins hung out in her stories, to the fright of all the children in earshot. What was worse, her description of all these horrible creatures were not reported secondhand. Puss Parker had actually been present for all the terrible happenings. Children listened in wonder that one person could possibly have been witness to so many dreadful events. And after an evening of being entertained by Aunt Puss, every child needed the comforting presence of an adult in the bed with him.

Aunt Puss told stories of gardens and chickens that died after a witch looked upon them, as well as tales of bewitched white calves who tried to choke children. Yet a few of her tales were humorous.

Such was the one involving wash pots which took place one cold evening, the same weather prevailing in nearly all of her stories.

As she recounted the wash pot tale, she always leaned forwards and reduced her voice to a hoarse but audible whisper. "I was by myself, when I heard this terrible racket out in the backyard. At first, I was too scared to look outside. But after awhile, I couldn't stand that fracas any longer. So I gathered my courage and eased out the back door.

"I would see well in the bright moonlight. And what I saw almost made me fall over! Two wash pots were having a fight! Each one backed off, got a running start, and slammed into the other one. Slam! Bam! Get knocked a-winding, get up and start over. Somebody had put a spell on them wash pots."

Aunt Puss told these tales to several generations, for she lived to a ripe old age. She frightened and entertained us all along the way.

He Died As He Lived

Joseph Thomas Rawlins liked women. In addition to his wife Katie, and Nancy Jane Parker, who bore him four illegitimate children, he is reported to have had quite a few others scattered around the surrounding farming community. An assignation with one of them cost him his life.

Not very far from where Rawlins lived, there dwelled a certain man by the name of John K. Brown. And about a mile from where Brown lived was a large field owned by John Cravey.

One hot July day in 1869, two of John Cravey's sons, Dan and Bob, were plowing in that field. Presently along came John K. Brown, who was their uncle by marriage, with a proposal that the two teenagers were unable to resist.

"Boys," he said. "How would you like to go see some girls?"

That sounded like a definite improvement on plowing in a hot field. So Brown and the two boys took off toward the home of a woman who had a "house," two girls, and a reputation for entertaining.

Brown was angry when he reached the house and discovered the woman already in the company of Joseph T. Rawlins. A quarrel ensued between the two men. It seemed for a time that Rawlins was getting the best of it. Then Brown grabbed a fence rail and hitting him across the head, left Joseph Thomas Rawlins dead in the woman's yard. A twenty-five dollar autopsy by Dr. Michael Durr determined that Rawlins had been killed by a severe blow to the head.

Brown quickly made tracks. A posse led by Rawlins's nephew, Duncan Cameron, followed him all the way to Pensacola, Florida. But they were too late. Brown had already boarded a boat bound for Mexico and was never again seen in Georgia.

Meanwhile, deprived of vengeance on the true murderer, the Rawlins clan pounced on the two Cravey boys. Dan and Bob Cravey were arrested. It was only after much pleading by sound heads that it was agreed that the boys' only crime was being in the wrong place at the wrong time.

But Joseph Thomas Rawlins, Jr. (Tom), youngest son of the murder victim, was not satisfied. He brooded over it for a while, and decided to get him a Cravey, younger brother of Dan and Bob. Knocking Henry in the head with a singletree, Rawlins left him for dead.

But Tom Rawlins was wrong in his assessment of the situation, for Henry Cravey was not dead. And in 1876 the latter married Eliza Parker, illegitimate half-sister of Tom Rawlins.

Some time after his marriage, Henry Cravey looked out the door and saw a figure approaching the house. "Put another plate on the table, Eliza," he said. "I think I see your brother Tom coming."

It was indeed Tom. He came in, sat and had a pleasant meal, put on his hat and left. All without saying anything about his earlier attempt to kill his host. After he had gone, Henry Cravey declared perplexedly to his wife, "I reckon that was Tom's way of apologizing."

Jonathan

Jonathan Studstill (the colored, or if one prefers, black one) fancied himself a songwriter, claiming authorship of several Negro gospel songs, including one entitled "You Gonna Want Somebody to Go Your Bond on Judgment Day." But it was within the white household of Levy and Caroline Garrison that Jonathan reached his greatest renown.

Levy and Jonathan had been childhood playmates and remained on a first name basis for the rest of their lives. Jonathan worked on the Garrison farm, but it was agreed that his biggest value was to the Garrison children whom he claimed to have "raised".

In the days when a small boy wore a dress or "apron" until he was about four years old, it was to Jonathan that Saxton Garrison went to show off his first pair of britches. Jonathan immediately took time out from work, and set Saxton up on a stump. Then he proceeded to walk all around that stump, admiring both the britches and the boy from every angle.

But Jonathan was not always so ready to build up an ego. He called a boy a "boy" and insisted that there were limits on what was proper for such a one to do. As the child increased in age, he became a "mankind," and as such was entitled to more privileges. Yet, he still was barred from activities reserved only for a "man".

For all of Jonathan's achievements, support, and understanding, Saxton Garrison still maintains that Jonathan's crowning accomplishment was the day that he saved the boy's teeth.

Saxton, a mischievous five-year-old, had bitten his little sister Mary. His father asked the boy if it was an accident or if he did it on purpose. Saxton knew that an accident was bad, whereas "purpose" was a new word with a nice ring to it. Eager to try the feel of it on his tongue, he announced that he had done it on purpose.

Whereupon, the boy's father turned to an older son and said, "Morgan, go get me a pair of pliers. It Saxton is going to use his teeth to bite his sister, then we'll just have to get shed of those teeth."

Jonathan, who up until now had remained quiet, then spoke up. "Levy, I'm acquainted with this boy here purty good. And I know, just as well as I know my own name that he's not ever going to bite his sister again. Please let him keep his teeth this time."

His father having agreed to spare his teeth, the small Saxton walked off, running his tongue over his teeth and thinking how fortunate he had been that Jonathan was there to save him.

Don't Pull Your Own Wagon

Jerry Rawlins, grandson of Joseph and Katie Rawlins, operated a cotton gin, located at the bottom of a quite steep hill on the Rawlins farm.

In the thick of cotton-ginning season one of Jerry Rawlins's friends died; and ginning operations were suspended long enough for Rawlins to attend the funeral. Meanwhile, a good number of wagons were lined up waiting for the gin to resume operations, when the Durden brothers appeared on the scene with a load of cotton.

Identical in appearance, they were small men, clad in overalls, no shoes, and sporting long beards. They surveyed the situation, and seeing that they had a long wait, decided to unhitch their wagon at the top of the hill, where their mules could enjoy the cool of several large shade trees.

Presently, Rawlins resumed ginning cotton, and the Durden brothers decided that it was time to pull their wagon into line. But, they reasoned, there was not need to hitch their mules back up for such a short pull. After all, it was downhill all the way. So they would just move the wagon themselves.

51

One brother took hold of the wagon tongue. Thus he would steer, while his brother would push on the back of the vehicle. In such manner they started downhill.

And downhill they went. Faster and faster and faster. With the speeding wagon pushing him harder from behind, the brother in front found it impossible to maintain either control of the wagon or his footing. Soon he tripped over a tree root and fell sprawling. The wagon passed over him; and his fallen figure tripped the brother who was still pushing diligently from behind.

It did not take long for it to become quite evident that both brothers were decidedly cross, for their fists were flying—at each other. Tom Gore rescued their runaway wagon and placed it in the ginning line, while the other bystanders found that this was a good opportunity to enjoy a truly spectacular fight.

Levi (Levy) Wright Garrison and wife, Caroline Cravey Garrison

The Not-Quite-Family Bible

Things were busy at the home of Levy and Caroline Garrison. They were preparing for an important weekend house guest, the Methodist preacher. In those days when the Methodists had church services only once a month, it was the custom for families in the congregation to take turns hosting the minister, who was usually not a local resident. On such occasions, a family tried to make a good impression with a clean house, well behaved children, and good Sunday cooking.

Caroline Garrison supervised the scrubbing of the wooden floors with lye soap and a corn shuck broom. She had baked cakes; and several roosters had been visually earmarked for the frying pan. The children had been warned not to talk out of turn, grab the best pieces of chicken, or, heaven forbid, pick their noses.

Late on Friday afternoon, when Caroline surveyed the situation, she was mostly pleased. Everything seemed to be up to snuff—with one exception. Knowing that the visiting preacher would surely want to read from the family Bible, she had placed it in a prominent place. And it just wouldn't do, for the Book was frayed around the edges, and, what was worse, it had a couple of torn pages.

"We ought to have already seen about getting a new one," she muttered to herself. "But it's too late now."

But wait a minute! Maybe it wasn't too late to obtain a new just-for-the-weekend Bible. She had just remembered Minnie Stynchcombe. Minnie, a "colored" woman, who lived down the road, had "nice" things, among which, Caroline Garrison remembered, was a beautiful Bible.

Hurriedly, one of the older children was sent to the Stynchcombe house to ask Minnie for a short loan of her Bible. Soon it was done, and the fine Book placed on the center table in the front room.

After supper, the Garrisons sat in that room waiting for Brother Domingoes to lead the family worship. The minister took the Bible from its resting place, turned it in his hands appreciatively, and opened it to ... the portion of the Book reserved for family records, where his eye fell on Stynchcombe marriages, Stynchcombe births, and Stynchcombe deaths.

Puzzled, Brother Domingoes looked up and a red-faced Caroline Garrison hastened to explain why the fine Book, which he had taken from her center table, was not exactly the Garrison Family Bible.

The Revival Nightmare

Most crops were "laid by" by the latter part of July, and it was not time to start picking cotton. So that was the time Mt. Zion Methodist Church usually chose for a week-long revival, with services morning and evening.

One summer Levy Garrison's family was to host the minister, along with the visiting speaker. Caroline was prepared to do her usual job of cooking, cleaning, and whatever else a good hostess is called upon to do. And her son, Saxton, was very pleased to help her. Anything to miss the revival.

Not that he was against church. He was a regular attendant. But revivals were quite different. The preaching was fine. The music was the problem.

The songs in the hymnal were comfortable and safe. But during revivals, folks tended to get beside themselves and bring on "special music." That got frightening close to "Gospel Sings."

Saxton hadn't been to one of those things since the time when his father, who liked such goings-on, had taken his small son along with him to a "sing." Saxton found himself trapped in among a group of clapping hands and stomping feet that belonged to BIG folks, who seemed called upon to back up the singing with their home–grown noise. After he finally managed to escape that jungle of hands and feet, he made his way to a window and jumped out. And he made up his mind to never again be in the building with a "Gospel Sing."

You could never really trust what singers might do at a revival. The very thought made him feel like climbing the walls, jumping out a window, or staying home to slop the hogs or milk the cows. Playing sick would be a little harder to pull off. But this time, he didn't have a thing to worry about. Staying home to help his mother play hostess was safe. It even made him feel a little holy. Here he was, making a sacrifice working for the good of the church. Maybe God would notice.

But Saxton did not know what he had let himself in for. Neither did his mother.

The problem arose when, without forewarning, the visiting speaker brought along his wife and a big herd of young'uns. And none of them attended the services.

As Saxton recalled:

That preacher's wife didn't do anything except "nuss" her baby. And that bunch of wild young'uns spent their time running amok. They were here; they were there; they were everywhere they shouldn't have been. And doing everything they weren't supposed to do. They broke every dessert dish Ma had.

I really wanted to bop a few of them up side their heads as a warning to the others, but I knew that Ma and Pa would seriously frown on that. So I just kept on helping Ma being run off her feet trying to prevent housekeeping from being broken up to such an extent that we would never be able to fix it.

By the end of the week, there were enthusiastic reports of the success of the revival. There was even talk of extending the services for another week.

I was listening when Ma told Pa, "If this revival lasts another week, I'm running away from home".

Fortunately, the revival ended at the originally scheduled time. And Ma didn't go amiss.

Weddings

In the old days, many weddings were held in the home of the bride's parents. Family and friends were invited to share a meal afterward.

In 1885, a double wedding was scheduled at the home of Joshua and his wife, Mary Jane Boney Cravey. Two of their daughters, Elizabeth (Liz) and Jane were to marry Samuel Luke McDuffie (Luke) and his brother James (Jim), sons of Samuel McDuffie and his wife, Amelia Rawlins.

Jim and Jane were married in the morning as planned. Luke announced that he wasn't quite ready. The call came for dinner, at which time Liz declared that she would never eat again until she was married to Luke. He remarked, "In that case, you'll be a mighty cheap woman to keep," and proceeded to fill his plate.

There are no reports about whether Liz actually ate anything. But it is known that when Luke left to go home, she went with him. Their son, Joseph Clayton, was born in 1886.

By the time the baby was old enough to become quite mobile, the neighbor men paid Luke a visit. "Marry Liz or, when the grand jury meets again, we'll get a bill against you."

Apparently, Luke McDuffie decided that the bonds of matrimony were less confining than jailhouse bars. So one April morning he and Liz brought their baby over to the neighboring Garrison home, before setting off in search of a Justice of the Peace.

Levy Garrison, age 11, was given the job of minding Baby Clayton, whose main goal seemed to be "getting into everything." He was described as a "fast little booger" by Levy, who found himself running all over the house, getting that toddler out of this, that, and the other.

In those days, little young'uns, no matter their gender, wore long gowns. That gave Levy Garrison an idea.

He picked up little Clayton, took him to a bed, and lifted up the bedpost. Then he stuck the hem of the toddler's garment under the post, which he then lowered back into place. This restricted Clayton's playground to a small area around the bed.

No one ever reported how long it took for Luke and Liz McDuffie to get safely married. But it would not be an exaggeration to say that for little Clayton it was much too long.

In 1916 a wedding took place in which the groom was not at all reluctant. The same could not be said for his in-laws.

Mr. Frank Smith, an expert craftsman, had been hired to do some construction at the neighboring Levy Garrison farm. It was probably a flower pit, for Caroline Garrison was quite partial to such things. As her son Saxton recalled:

When Ma got dinner ready, she sent me out to tell Mr. Smith to come eat. I told him three times, but he just kept on working, and never even answered. So I went back and reported the situation to Ma.

So she came out and said, "Mr. Smith, I've got dinner on the table."

He burst into tears. "Miz Caroline, I never want to eat another mouthful as long as I live."

"What in the world is wrong?"

"My Exie ran off and got married last night."

Then he reminded Ma how his older daughter had moved with her new husband up around the Georgia-Tennessee line, and died when her first baby was born.

"I don't have anything against my new son-in-law. Joel Spires is all right. But I'm afraid for my other girl to get married."

Of course, Ma sympathized with him.

After she had consoled him for a while, he dried his tears, went in the house with us, and ate a big dinner.

I figured that sympathy must make folks have a better appetite.

Charlie Y. Walker saw the prospect of his daughter marrying quite differently than Mr. Smith viewed the marriage of his Exie.

After he mustered out of the army at the end of World War I, Frank Thompson left his hometown of Eatonton, and came to Telfair County. He and Alice Walker, oldest child of Charlie and Mary Cravey Walker, started courting and decided to marry.

When the prospective bride's father got that word, he pondered on what he should do with it. He sat looking out the window, and saw his old horse, Henry, munching away in the pasture. Then he knew!

If Paul Revere rode to give an alarm, Charlie Walker could ride to tell good news. Soon Mr. Walker swung himself into the saddle and raced to the nearest neighbor's house.

"Alice is gonna get married, but don't tell a soul," he confided.

Then he rode hell-for-leather to the next neighbor with the same announcement and admonishment to keep quiet about it. "Alice is gonna get married, but don't tell a soul."

So it went for the rest of the day. Race old Henry, give the wedding announcement, and swear everyone to secrecy.

Before it was over, all friends and family had been informed of the upcoming nuptials. All delivered by the bride's father, who had managed to maintain an exclusive on this news story.

Some of the neighbors noticed that old Henry seemed lethargic for a few days, almost as if her were too tired to graze.

A black man named Will Sims, had also served in World War I. And he, too, had decided to get married. He and his sweetheart, Charlotte Moten, went over to the home of Lochlin Morris Cravey, who was the nearest Justice of the Peace.

After he had performed the marriage ceremony, Mr. Cravey turned to the groom and said, "You may now salute the bride."

Whereupon ex-soldier Sims gave a crisp and perfect military salute.

"Kiss her, you crazy fool," Mr. Cravey commanded.

Will Sims did as ordered.

Going to Town

Small towns were a lot more active in the early days of the 1900's than they are today. There were more stores and certainly more excitement. At least in Milan, anything could happen.

Jasper Rawlins could walk from his home in the Sandhill Church Community all the way to Milan. And he walked fast.

As he walked past the home of his cousins Levy and Caroline Garrison, she would say, "Well, I reckon Jasper has run out of his dope."

The "dope" was paregoric, an opium syrup, which though closely regulated nowadays was then an over-the-counter product. It was used for the treatment of bellyaches, fretful or teething babies, or for any other reason a person chose.

Once Mr. Rawlins bought his "dope" (and presumably took a few swigs), he strolled back home in a leisurely fashion.

Patsy Cravey Smith also walked a fast clip on her way to Milan. Her cousin, Betsy Cravey Williams, out working in her flower bed, saw her and was puzzled.

"Patsy, where are you going in such a hurry?" she called out.

Patsy only slightly reduced her speed, and answered, "Going to see about Sister Fannie Mae. The water tower has fallen on her."

"How do you know that?"

The tone of Patsy's answer was one reserved for those who ask stupid questions. "Didn't you hear that big noise awhile ago?"

"Oh Patsy, that was just some farmer blasting out stumps with a charge of dynamite".

Patsy was unconvinced and trotted on off toward Milan.

This action poses several questions. 1. Why was the noise assigned to the water tower? 2. What motive or grudge drove the water tower to choose Fannie Mae to fall upon? 3. Why did Fannie Mae cooperate by standing under the water tower, thus putting herself in position to be squashed?

However, maybe those questions are irrelevant. Perhaps the best answer to Patsy's quick–stepping trip was that she simply wanted to visit her sister. (Fannie Mae had recently married Paul Parker and moved to Milan.) It has been said that a poor excuse is better than none.

Sunday was set aside for going to church. Just so, Saturday was the usual day for going to town. Every Saturday afternoon, farmers streamed into town. For the most part wives didn't go; the men bought the groceries. And there were other things to do besides shopping.

There was often the opportunity to watch a fight (or to take part in one). Sometimes there was even a murder. But to be fair, most men preferred to limit themselves to observation, rather than be a party to murder.

In an anything-may-happen atmosphere, Saxton Garrison was not surprised to see a big farm truck park on the street and two unknown men approach him.

"Can you tell us how to get to Mt. Zion Church Cemetery?" the taller one asked.

"Sure," Saxton replied, and started giving directions.

The shorter man stopped him. "Actually, we have a body to bury there. And we need a member of that church to choose the place for us to put it. We don't want that responsibility. Is there a member of that church around here?"

"I'm a member of Mt. Zion," Saxton stated. "But I'm not going to pick out a place for a grave site without another member's help. I see Buster Lancaster across the street. Maybe I can get him to go out there with me."

So Buster and Saxton led the strangers' truck out to Mt. Zion and picked out a place for them to dig a grave. Then the two of them went back to Milan.

Years later, Saxton attempted to show someone where the grave site was. There was no marker. Neither was there a mound of dirt denoting an unmarked grave.

Saxton was asked who was buried there. He didn't know.

Was it possible (even likely) that Saxton and Buster had helped the mob dispose of a murder victim's body? Or were the proceeds of a robbery buried in the cemetery that evening?

It is not known if Buster was even interviewed on the subject. But when these questions were posed to Saxton, he only smiled.

Truly, anything could happen around Milan. Especially on Saturday.

Milan vs. Rhine

From the very beginning of the development of the towns of Milan and Rhine with the coming of the railroad in the late 1880s, there was always a running discussion about which town was meaner.

Those voting for Milan would point out that when the first trains came through, the conductor cautioned each passenger to "duck" upon entering Rhine. But they claimed that as the train pulled into Milan, his admonition strengthened to, "Get under the seat."

Those giving Milan first place in the "mean" contest further pointed out its 1919 lynching of George Washington for the murder of John Dowdy. And they further called attention to the aftermath of the lynching, when some folks out on the County Line Road sent word through the switchboard that they were coming in to kill Homer Stuckey, the policeman who had stood out unsuccessfully against the lynch mob. Furthermore, the warning continued, Milan would be completely torn apart. And when Jim Pace came into John Cravey's store waving a pistol, it seemed that the threats were about to be carried out.

Those insisting that Milan was not as some folks would like to claim, argue that the threat of this riot was all sound and fury, greatly exaggerated, and that when Homer Stuckey arrested Pace for disturbing the peace that the policeman couldn't even find a gun on the man. Tom Cravey (called Crooked-Armed Tom to differentiate him from Button-Head Tom and Clay Root Tom), who was in the store at the time, privately maintained that Pace had had a gun, which he had quickly shoved down into a barrel of dried peas just before he was arrested.

At any rate, the riot died a-borning; and that, in itself, is cited as proof that Milan was not nearly as bad as was claimed.

Furthermore, some people feel that Rhine's unofficial "mean man" contest puts that town way out front as the roughest place.

Rhine has had, over the years, several men who people have claimed as "the meanest man in the world," but many have maintained that Tom Burnam was the meanest of all. Burnam was so dreaded, according to one story, that when a man from Hawkinsville, Georgia, found himself in a Mississippi town and quite without funds, he walked into a saloon, announced that his name was Tom Burnam, and was immediately supplied with sufficient money with which to return to Rhine. Burnam was said to be so mean that when he was gunned down by a fourteen year old boy in downtown Rhine, his killer was congratulated by the community for a job well done.

But as rough as Burnam was, many of the activities of John Stuckey were cited as proof that he was meaner. Stuckey was said to be a man who neglected to remember that the Emancipation Proclamation meant no more slavery.

One man known for general cussedness was Bill Pickren, who owned at one time, a field in the center of which was located the old Campbell Family Cemetery. Pickren, it was said, got drunk one day during corn planting season and took a dislike to that cemetery. So he plowed up the road giving access to the burying ground traffic and planted corn in the furrows. But before he quite finished planting, he found that he needed to ride into Rhine for supplies. On the trip back home, his horse shied; and the gun he was wearing fired off, severing his femoral artery. Thus Bill Pickren became the first corpse to be hauled into the Campbell Cemetery across plowed up ground.

In spite of all the evidence cited, there is still general disagreement as to the true identity of Rhine's meanest man, just as for most folks, it has never been decided for sure which of the two towns most deserved the meanness award.

As the years went by, the rivalry between Milan and Rhine became less acute. However, one old man sitting on a bench in Milan still had the roughest-toughest contest in his mind, and was firm in his conclusion about the identity of the winner.

There was a peculiar thing about the benches and the sitters on them. No one can name the exact time when it happened, but a stable pattern had been reached. What used to be a bench in front of nearly every store had become a bench every now and then. At the same time, there were also less folks needing or wanting to sit on the available benches. When one bench sitter died, another just entering his dotage stepped up to take his place. It was almost as if there was some balancing agent at work.

Most bench sitting took place on Saturday afternoons, but a few dedicated men had a habit of meeting for bench sitting every morning (except Sunday). Three of them regularly grouped themselves together on the bench in front of Cook's Grocery, day after day after day.

On a certain morning one of them appeared at their meeting place looking quite glum.

"Why are you so down-in-the-mouth?" the second man asked.

"Just been listening to the radio," was the reply. "And the news from across the water ain't good."

"What happened?"

"Them Germans have gone and crossed the Rhine."

"Could it be that the radio was right?" said the third man, who was a bit hard of hearing. "But I ain't gonna worry nothing a-tall about it. Them Germans may have crossed through Rhine. But they'll never make it through Milan!"

The Strong Arm of the Law

One Saturday afternoon during the time that Dave Cravey (son of George Troup Cravey and Ellen Reaves) and Bob Yawn were policing Milan, a certain prominent local farmer came into town after having imbibed a little too much of the hard stuff. Wishing lighter refreshment than that of which he had recently partaken, he strode up to the soda fountain in Dr. Clark's drugstore and ordered a root beer.

The trouble arose because the farmer had forgotten to wear pants. The two policemen held a hurried consultation and agreed that a man without pants should be speedily returned to the countryside from whence he had come.

Bob Yawn marched boldly up and tapped the sipping gentleman on the shoulder. Whereupon, without much apparent effort, the farmer picked Yawn up and tossed him swiftly out the window.

Policeman Cravey, remembering the old adage, "Fools rush in where angels fear to tread," probably did not consider himself an angel. But neither was he about to play the fool.

"By Jinx, boys," he announced, "I've got to go feed my horse."

And he left the underwear-clad gentleman at the soda fountain to drink his root beer in peace.

The Rawlins-Carter Feud

Not far from the grave of Lucius Williams in Blockhouse Churchyard is the tombstone of J.G. Rawlins. Upon reading the extraordinary inscription carved on its face, one wonders immediately what unusual story lies behind such an epitaph.

Joseph Gooden Rawlins was the only son of James and Polly Williams Rawlins. Growing up in Telfair County, Joe became friends with a boy by the name of W.L. Carter.

After the boys were grown and married, a quarrel arose between them over twelve hogs which Carter claimed that Rawlins had stolen. According to one source, Carter later admitted that he himself had sold the hogs.

Rawlins had married Angeline Jowers from the section around the Coffee County town of Ambrose. And it was to this area that he moved in an attempt to avoid Carter.

However, W.L. Carter was a hard man to lose. He bought a farm adjacent to the Rawlins land in Coffee County. And when Rawlins, his wife, and three sons moved to Lowndes County, Carter bought land separated from the Rawlins farm by only a ten acre strip.

He later had strong reason to deeply regret having followed Rawlins, for on the night on June 13, 1906, a terrible thing happened at the Carter homestead. The horror occurred at the hands of a black man by the name of Alf Moore. But there have been several stories circulated about exactly how and why he committed such a crime.

Moore claimed at first that he acted alone and at his own instigation. Later he stated that he had been hired by J. G. Rawlins and his two oldest sons to kill the Carter family.

The only members of the Carter family who were actually murdered were two children, ages 13 and 16. One account of their killing alleges that Moore, hiding in the darkness outside the Carter home, shot at the first human figures to emerge from the house, even though he did not at all recognize his targets.

But there is a much more horrible version of this killing. This story claims that Moore went to the scene of the crime intent on killing Mr. Carter, who, when called, refused to emerge from the house.

Then, in an attempt to lure Carter outside, Moore walked into the barn and into the livestock pens, creating uproar among the animals. Yet Carter steadfastly remained inside the house.

But two of the Carter children, upon hearing the terrified bleats of their pet calves, ran outside to their doom. For, according to this account of the tragedy, Moore caught the children and tortured them in an effort to compel their father to come to their rescue. But W. L. Carter never came; and by morning both of the children were dead.

This version of the murder places two of the sons of J.G. Rawlins at the scene of the crime, and states that Rawlins, himself, spent the evening of June 13 in downtown Valdosta. This story goes on to declare that his companion for the evening was the Sheriff of Lowndes County.

Whatever the truth about the motive for this crime, or the method by which it was committed, it cost the lives of not only the two Carter children, but the lives of Alf Moore and Joseph Gooden Rawlins as well. For those two men were hanged in December in 1906.

The two Rawlins sons were given life sentences. However, in a few years, their grandfather, Jonathan Jowers, was able to persuade the governor to free them both.

Many people in Telfair County doubted the guilt of either the Rawlins boys or their father. Here there was strong talk among the Rawlins kin about the best method of storming the Valdosta jail and rescuing them. But plans for the jailbreak never came to fruition. And perhaps that is fortunate, for the Valdosta lawmen, it has been said, were prepared for just such an attempt and were well equipped to quell it. So Joseph Gooden Rawlins was hanged, and his body returned to Telfair County from whence it had come.

The guilt of this man is still questioned in the minds of some people. But to the author of his epitaph, (said to be Rawlins himself), it seems a settled fact, for carved on the tombstone of J.G. Rawlins are these words:

This bark was well
built but misguided,
run swift on the rocks
of destruction.

South Carolina Puzzles

One year when Saxton Garrison was a teenager, his father made a bumper crop of cotton. The problem was that there were not enough hands to pick it.

Then word got out that, up in the hills of South Carolina, there were a lot of people out of work.

As Saxton recalled:

Pa loaded himself and me into a big farm truck, and we took off for South Carolina. We rolled into a little hill town along late in the afternoon. Pa went into a store and declared his business. The store keeper said, "You're in luck. I see Mr. Green across the street. He says that a lot of folks in his neck of the woods can't find work. Why don't you step over there and speak a word to him"?

We got a good reception from Mr. Green. "I can get you all the hands you want. But it's getting right late in the day. I 'spect it'll be nigh on to dark by the time we can get to my house."

He pushed his big old hat back and scratched his head. "Tell you what. Why don't you come home with me, and spend the night? Then in the morning I can load you up with everybody you need."

If there was a better deal than that, Pa didn't seem to know what it was. So soon we were following Mr. Green along winding dirt roads until, about the edge of dark, we pulled up in front of a big old ramshackle house. It was nothing to brag on, but it did seem to have plenty of room for spend-the-night company.

The welcome we got was royal. Soon we were sitting down to a table and the rations were being passed around.

The Greens had several children, the oldest one, about my age, was called Junior. I was too busy watching him even to pay attention to what we were eating. He kept our plates and glasses filled. He acted like he was training to be a butler. Not that I had actually seen one of those. But I have heard that they are cool, dignified and rather stiff. Junior Green was not like that. He smiled a lot, and seemed to be always dipping or pouring something. I decided that he was probably a little too perky to make it as a butler. Whatever he was trying to do, he stuck to the same solicitous style. Carrying a kerosene lamp, he led us to a big room with a double bed. He practically tucked us in.

When he left with the lamp, it was awfully dark. Soon I started to doze off. Then Pa poked me in the ribs.

"There's somebody in this room," he whispered. "I've got a purty good roll of money on me, and I'm not going to lie here and be robbed."

I listened and there did seem to be someone quietly stirring around in the room. Had Junior Green's friendliness been setting us up for a robbery?

"I noticed some wood in the fireplace," Pa continued. "I'm going to ease over there and get me a stick. When I give you a sign, you strike a match." With that, he shoved a little matchbox into my hands.

Another poke in my ribs, and I quickly lit a match as fast as I could.

In the dim light, we saw a big, a huge, a monstrous wharf rat moving around the room!

Junior appeared to be innocent of robbery plans. But I couldn't figure out what he was up to. What was motivating him? Maybe he was gearing up to be a politician.

The next morning, loaded up with cotton pickers, Pa and I struck out for home. And I left the puzzle of Junior Green behind.

We also left the wharf rat in South Carolina.

Benjamin Hezekiah Davis and wife Abbie Hunter Davis
(Photograph courtesy Betty Lynn McRae Johnson,
their granddaughter)

A Good Woman

Abbie Hunter Davis was the wife of Ben Davis who lived in the China Hill area of Telfair County. "Aunt Abbie" as she was known around the neighborhood, never called her husband by his first name. He was always "Mr. Davis" to her.

She had grown up in Ben Hill County in a family who taught that a woman must never call her husband by his given name. And Aunt Abbie always did what she was supposed to do.

She was a slender, dark-haired woman with big brown eyes. She was rather attractive in spite of her style of dress, which, on most days, was a long cotton dress set off by high-topped tennis shoes.

Late one afternoon, she crossed the branch, and walked the short distance to the home of her husband's sister, Annie Mae Ray.

"I'm worried," she confided. "Mr. Davis went to the river swamp fishing early this morning, and he's not come home. Annie Mae, do you reckon somebody has knocked Mr. Davis in the head and taken his pocketbook?"

No one had.

On another occasion, the Davis and Ray families had ridden together in a horse-drawn wagon to Bethel Methodist Church for a revival meeting. It was hot weather, and since the church was cooled only by hand-held cardboard fans, most people stood in groups in the relatively cooler churchyard until time for the service to begin.

While Aunt Abbie and Annie Mae Ray stood chatting, a large bug interrupted their conversation. He flew fast and high up under Aunt Abbie's dress. She instinctively gave her crotch a slap. Then she blushed all the way to the roots of her hair.

That prim and proper woman turned with dismay to her sister-in-law. "Oh, Annie Mae, do you reckon those men over there thought I was making a sign to them?"

Motivated to Move

Archie McCrimmon learned a mighty valuable lesson one bright morning in late October: no matter how big a mess you're in, you can get out of it, if you see something worse coming at you.

In those olden days, there were no four wheelers to ride through the woods, so many folks rode mules instead. Archie was peacefully riding his own mule, his red hair and beard combining with the oranges, reds, and yellows of the changing leaves to make a colorful woodland scene. He was feeling good, anticipating a meeting with a friend to set up some secret business plans.

But he soon found his way barred by an irate fella also riding a mule. This was a man who often had contrary plans to those of Mr. McCrimmon, and they had tangled in the past. In Archie's opinion, the fella needed a good whipping, and his big McCrimmon fists, which had served him well in the past, itched to deliver that beating. Archie's philosophy was that a good fist fight could go a long ways toward solving most any problem.

But alas! The unarmed McCrimmon saw that the other man was toting a gun. He did not, at this point, seem much inclined to use it, but fell into using his tongue instead. He began cussing Archie, calling vile attention to the general *sorriness* of the whole McCrimmon clan. He shouted obscenities that Archie, who was not ignorant of profane vocabulary, had never heard used before. (Archie filed them all in his memory for possible future use himself.)

He silently berated himself for having neither gun nor large cudgel with which to defend himself. But he was a true McCrimmon, and refused to appear scared. He stared belligerently at the other fella and said, "Well, if you're going to shoot me, go ahead and get it over with."

The other man refueled his mouth with cuss words. He cussed.

And he kept cussing.

After awhile, Archie said, "Tell you what I'm going to do. I'm going to turn my mule around and ride off. Then you can shoot me in the back, since you don't have enough nerve to shoot me to my face."

Soon after so, Archie got a big surprise. He had thought the other fella really wouldn't shoot off anything but his mouth. But he felt a shot go through his coat and strike him right where his galluses crossed in the back.

Of course he was knocked off his mule and seriously injured. But by some miracle, he was not only still alive, but conscious as well.

As he later told it, "I was bleeding and hurting real bad. I wondered how long it would take for somebody to find me, and if I would still be alive when they did. Then I looked up and saw two great big wild hogs a-coming.

"I couldn't get back on my mule. He was scared off by the shot, and long gone away. I started to crawl, and looking at them big sows a-coming, I found that I could crawl real fast. You'd be surprised how much get-up–and-go you can get from the thoughts of being eaten by two big hogs."

Jack Daniels to the Rescue

Alex Boney never had any use for sweet foods. He ate a piece of pie once, he said, and it made him so sick that he never put another sweet thing in his mouth. However, Mr. Boney did have an appreciation for good whiskey. Not that he was given to heavy drinking, but he always maintained that a bottle of quality stuff in the right place at the right time was a wonderful thing. The fact was, he declared, it once saved him from getting a good whipping.

The incident started in Mr. Boney's country store when he was exercising his considerable wit at the expense of the new Baptist preacher. The preacher wasn't in the store at the time, but an appreciative audience was. And Methodist Mr. Boney was enjoying pointing out the ridiculous deficiencies of the absent preacher. Among those listening to the storekeeper's fun was Mr. John Roberson.

As Mr. Boney later reported: "The next morning I looked out the door, and there coming toward the store was John Roberson riding in the buggy with Mose Williams, who was a died-in-the-wool Baptist. I knew he was crazy about that new preacher, and I knew that John Roberson had told him what I had said the day before. It also came to me right quick that Mose might want to whip me for laughing at his preacher. What was worse, I knew he could do it!

"But I thought fast, ran back in the store, felt down in a barrel of peas and came out with a bottle of Jack Daniels. Grabbing a glass, I ran out the door just as Mose was getting out of his buggy.

"Mose, my friend," I said. "I've got something I want you to try." And I handed him a glass of that whiskey.

"Purty good stuff?" I asked as he raised the glass to his lips.

He agreed that it was; and I shoved the bottle into his hand.

"Here, take it," I said. "It's yours, free of charge."

As he drove off with that whiskey, I yelled out, "But don't let John Roberson have a damned drop!"

Black as Pitch and Smells Like Collards

J.R. is not really his name. He insisted that his name, as well as all the other names in this story, be changed. He likes to spin yarns, but there was always a peculiar secrecy streak in J.R. So his terms were agreed to and here is his tale:

I don't ever smell collards without thinking about Cousin Leroy. Leroy was a real sport. He was right bad to drink, but at first that didn't matter to me. He was three years older than me, and had started letting me ride with him in his pa's old truck. So I thought he was the very trick.

Leroy had come along after his folks had raised a passel of girls. I don't think they ever knew what to do with a boy that was a little on the wild side.

He like to take a little swig and drive off lickety split down the County Line Road. It was just dirt back then, and in dry weather, it developed little ruts that made it like a washboard. And if the county wasn't right smart about pulling the ditches, a big rain would make a slurry of mud on the clay spots. Then the tires would sink down and cut deep ruts that would stay after the weather dried off. Driving that road was a bad job even for a sober man.

But when Leroy got about half-lit and went flying down the road, kicking up dirt and running over chickens, it was a thrilling experience to be riding with him.

After we had run in the gully a time or two, and I had gotten pretty skinned up, I said, "Leroy, if I go anywhere else with you, I'm a-driving." Course, I wasn't old enough for a driver's license, but back then folks didn't pay much attention to that.

Along in the early spring, the time when folks were trying to break land, it got a little too wet to plow for a day or two. That's when Leroy got after me to spend the night at his house and go fishing with him early the next morning.

"We'll go to the mouth of Horse Creek. And I'll let you drive."

So I walked over to Leroy's house with him, and we got there just as Aunt Sadie has finished getting supper on the table. We had collards, fried ham, crackling bread, with red-eye gravy to pour over baked sweet potatoes. After we ate us a bate, Leroy said, "Let's go outdoors."

I knew what that meant. Aunt Sadie was bad against drinking, so Leroy kept his booze hidden in the corn crib. He took a swig or two and then offered me the jug. But I turned it down because I didn't doubt that if I drank any, Pa would catch me. I declare that man could find out what I'd done before I'd ever done it. And I didn't doubt that if he caught me drinking, I'd turn out skinned up worse than if Leroy had driven me into the gully.

So I just said, "No, thank you, I don't believe I care for any."

After Leroy had him a few snorts, we went to bed. But before we got to sleep it started to thunder and lightning. We heard rain pounding on the tin roof. Then it started blowing in through the windows which had no glass. Shutters were used to keep out varmints and rain when necessary. So Leroy got up and closed the shutters, which greatly increased the darkness in the room.

"Aw, shucks," Leroy said. (Actually shucks, wasn't the word he used, but some ladies might read this.) "If that rain keeps up, we won't catch a thing tomorrow. When a fish gets rained on too much, he won't bite."

It rained right hard and steady a good while. When it stopped, Leroy said, "Maybe it's done broke off. There's too many trees on this side of the house to get a good look at the sky. But you can see real good from the kitchen windows. And they face the southwest where most of the bad storms come from. I believe I'll ease in there, open a shutter and look outside".

In those days people around here didn't have electric lights. But Leroy, having lived in this house all his life, knew his way through the hall, and was able to make his way to the kitchen in the dark. But I knew that I couldn't, so I stayed put.

In a couple of minutes I heard a loud yell from Leroy. "A bad storm's a-coming! A bad storm's a-coming!"

I just stood there, not knowing what to do. In those days, I was not as brave as I am now.

I saw Aunt Sadie go by with a kerosene lamp. I reckoned Uncle Walter was sleeping through the commotion, on account of his being right hard of hearing.

I fell in behind Aunt Sadie, following her white gown tail swishing along toward the kitchen. The shutters were all closed, the room lit only by the lamp she held.

There stood Leroy, jumping up and down, blinking his eyes, and looking stupid. Bless his heart, it was not hard for him to look that-a way.

He was hollering, "Lord have mercy! It's black as pitch and smells like collards!" Aunt Sadie looked right mean at him and said, "Leroy! You're as drunk as a coot! You've done gone and stuck your head in the pie safe where I put that bowl of leftover collards. Get yourself to bed!"

Leroy went.

I followed him, relieved that the weather didn't really smell like collards.

Part II

Genealogy

Family Photographs

Great-Uncle Levy Garrison, Sr. and his family about 1901.

Front: Levy Garrison, Lydia Hulett Garrison, Bessie Garrison

Back: John (Bud) Garrison, David Lee Garrison, Lola Garrison, Carrie Garrison

(Photo courtesy of Nell Davis Harris, a great-granddaughter)

Ray family cousins

Seated, left to right: William Washington Ray (Billy) and his cousin, Joseph Benjamin Ray.

Standing left to right: John Henry Ray and Jordan Abner Ray.

John Henry, Jordan Abner and Joseph Benjamin were brothers. Billy was their double-first cousin.

Lula Mae Ray, daughter of William Washington (Billy) and Addie Mae (Annie Mae) Davis Ray. Photo circa 1912. (Author's collection)

Ben Ray (1917-1942), son of William Washington (Billy) Ray and Annie Mae Davis Ray. (Photo courtesy of Billie Gray Curtis Vaughn)

"Bulldog Dave" Cravey and Family

(Bulldog was a nickname given to differentiate him from all of the other Dave Craveys.)

Top Row, Right to Left: Dave Cravey, Jodie Dowdy Cravey, baby in Jodie's arms is Amanda Lou Cravey, Bessie Cravey Davis, baby in Bessie's arms is Lula Davis, Leila Cravey Wynn, Dora Ann Cravey, Clara Cravey, and Edgar Harris Davis, Jr.

Bottom Row, Left to Right: Robert Wynn, Cliff Cravey, David Davis, George Cravey, Lillie May Davis, Carrie Belle Cravey, Maggie Cravey, Cola Cravey

Edgar Harris Davis, Jr. and Robert Fulton Wynn were Dave Cravey's sons-in-law.

(Photograph courtesy of Ernest Ray, Jr.)

Edgar Davis, Jr., son of Edgar/Edward
Davis, Sr. and Mary Frances Davis.
(Photo courtesy of Ernest Ray, Jr.)

George Morris Williams, son of
Joseph Gooden Williams, father of
Andrew Williams.(Photo courtesy of
Myrtle Knight)

James C. Spires (1821-1907)
married into the Rawlins
family twice. His first wife
Mary, daughter of J. T. and
Catherine Harrell Rawlins, died
due to a fall from a horse after
being married only eight
months. Jim then married her
cousin, Mary Jane McDuffie
whose mother was the sister of
J. T. Rawlins. They produced a
large family before she died. He
then married Rebecca Pitts and
had another family. Jim Spires
a clever and innovative man
reportedly proud of his large
family, said, "I'm the root and
branch of the Spires genera-
tion." The large number of his
descendants in this area con-
firms that statement.

FAMILY TREES
(Nuts and All)

This book was originally intended to be purely an anecdotal history and not a genealogy. This writer intended to add just enough family background to identify present day families with historical characters.

But like the beginning of a fight, one thing leads to another. Looking for one family relationship uncovered an interesting detail about another, while sometimes the fact for which the search was initiated was never found.

Accurately outlining a family history is hard work and fraught with many opportunities for error. It is easy to accept what has been written by others and tedious and time consuming to search for oneself. But the latter is the only way the writer has any control over the accuracy of the material, for sometimes one pounces with glee on a book containing the very family about which a long search has been made, only to find that it contains errors. One quickly learns that genealogy is, at best, a difficult art. One searches books, court house and census records, interviews people, and then hopes to have a good sense not to misinterpret what has been found.

87

This writer has diligently endeavored to keep error at a minimum. Nevertheless, it is certain that mistakes are bound to be found within these covers.

(Note: Space and time did not permit the inclusion of subsequent generations of family lines in this book. Some such material, as well as data on other families, is in the possession of this author. This material will be shared with anyone who is interested.)

We Have Found the Melungeons and They Are Us

Initially, there was no intention to hunt Melungeons. The research was designed to look for Indians.

Many, if not most, people in the southeast have family stories about an Indian great-grandfather or a Cherokee great-great grandmother. Unfortunately details to substantiate such claims are flimsy. An attempt to find concrete evidence to support such stories on both sides of this researcher's maternal line brought to light the word "Melungeon."

What in the world is a Melungeon? An Indian word for deer meat stew? A new computer game set in the seventeenth century Appalachian Mountains? A secret Indian mound built by members of the lost tribe of Dan?

No, none of the above.

A Melungeon is a person whose genetic background is an ill defined ethnic mix. Where they came from and how they came to the Southeast is the subject of much debate, but little agreement. Until recently, Melungeons themselves usually denied that ethnic designation. Some would not even admit ever having seen such a person.

There is not room in this article (nor capability in this writer's head) to completely explain Melungeons. The Melungeon puzzle is better detailed in three books published by Mercer University Press in Macon, Georgia:

The Melungeons: The Resurrection of A Proud People; An Untold Story Of Ethnic Cleansing, by N. Brent Kennedy with Robyn Vaughan Kennedy, 1994, revised 1997.

Walking Toward the Sunset: The Melungeons of Appalachia, by Wayne Winkler, 2004

Melungeons: The Last Lost Tribe in America, by Elizabeth Caldwell Hirschman, 2005.

These volumes, written by Melungeons, do not fully agree on every clue or theory about who these people actually are. And census takers certainly didn't agree. The lighter-skinned ones may have been designated "white". Others were labeled "free persons of color", "mulatto", or a derogatory term long used to describe persons of African descent. The government clearly did not know how to categorize these people.

Melungeons usually have dark to medium reddish-brown complexion, but some are fair-skinned. Generally, they have fine European facial features, some with high cheekbones, but occasionally African American features such as a broad nose pops up. They have dark hair, except when they are blond or red–headed. Their eyes are dark, except when they are gray or blue. One thing does remain fairly constant among Melungeons: they tend to have English surnames.

Melungeons often describe themselves as "Portyghee" (Portuguese) or Indian. Some people have said that they were Turks, Crypto-Jews, Spaniards, Moors from Northern Africa, or of other exotic descent. In short, they seemed to be "everybody". But a Melungeon was usually treated as if he was "nobody". He was persecuted, maligned, and often pushed into areas where it was hard to make a living.

Yet, there are a number of well known and prosperous people, such as Elvis Presley, with Melungeon roots. Abraham Lincoln and Jefferson Davis have more in common than the American Civil War. Hirschman's book (pages 89-95) gives their supposed Melungeon backgrounds and shows their remarkably similar facial structure.

Although rumors of this author's Indian ancestry were recurrent and passionately recounted, research using many means and sources, did not lead to any concrete evidence of Indian ancestry. Explanations provided in the cited books suggest another possible ethnic origin for what have passed for Indian looks in the family. The Davises and Abbotts may be Melungeons, a "duke's mixture" of many ethnic pieces deriving from places of which one never dreamed, (of course, this does not rule out the possibility that Native American Indians were one of those pieces.) (See Davis and Abbott genealogies.)

Another conclusion roars loudly. People who see themselves at the end of a long genetic flow from a "pure" race, having no "taint" of genes from unacceptable locales, are almost certainly deluding themselves. Such a background, if it were likely, could be considered a bit bland, like a dish without seasoning. What some consider a "taint" may be looked upon as "spice".

Truly, Southerners are "fearfully and wonderfully made," but not from genetic ingredients that they would necessarily have chosen.

WILLIAMS, RAWLINS, BONEY, WELLS and Others

The Williams family who settled near Jacksonville, Georgia about 1823 were originally residents of Duplin County, North Carolina, and are said to be of Welsh origin. However, neither the route by which the first of this clan reached the coastal plains of North Carolina nor his exact identity, has yet been learned. Several people are working on this question, but, so far, there are not proven facts, only several logical theories. It is known that several families named Williams lived in Duplin County in the Pre-Revolutionary War days and that some of them seem to be closely associated. Many of these fox-hunting, dancing, fun-loving Presbyterians settled in the Rockfish Creek Area along with the Boney, Wells, Fussell, and Knowles Families.

Joseph Williams, who came to lower Telfair County, Georgia, along with all his children, is believed to be the second son of a father with that same name. However, the surplus of Joseph Williamses in Duplin County makes definite identification rather difficult. There were: the man we know as Joseph Sr.; his son Joseph Jr.; Joseph, the son of John Williams, who is believed to be the brother of Joseph Sr.; the Joseph Williams who served as a member of both the North Carolina House of Commons and as the Duplin County Sheriff, and Joseph Williams, the Tavern Keeper. (In addition, there were several Johns and Stephens plus a couple of Byrds, all with the surname Williams.)

Tradition states that PHOEBE LITTLE was wife of the JOSEPH WILLIAMS SR., who was born about 1735, and died about 1791. But there is no concrete evidence to support this assertion. On the contrary, deeds assigned in 1779, by Joseph Williams Sr., and his wife, show that Mary was her name. These deeds were made to their sons, Aaron and Joseph Jr., and can be found in Sampson-Duplin Deed Book 6, pages 301 and 319.

CHILDREN OF JOSEPH WILLIAMS, SR.:

1. AARON, 1757-1808, married MARY NEWTON, daughter of ISSAC NEWTON. Aaron was a captain in the Duplin County Militia during the Revolutionary War.

2. JOSEPH, JR., 1759-1850, is buried, along with large numbers of descendants, in the Blockhouse Churchyard on Highway 117 near Jacksonville, Ga. (This church began in a blockhouse or fort built against Indian attack, and remains a very active church to this day.) His

DAR monument states that he was a lieutenant in the Revolution. (He received a military pension from 1833 until 1844, when during the race for Telfair County Clerk of Superior Court, James McCall publicly stated that he would have Williams' pension cut off. As a result, there was a gap in Mr. Williams' pension checks, for he had to reapply and furnish witnesses to his military service.) Various sources have given Joseph's wife as NANCY EVANS, MARY ERVIN, and MEALY BEVIN. In spite of the confusion generated by the large number of Joseph Williamses, this researcher is firmly convinced that MEALY BEVIN, who married Joseph Williams in 1780, was the wife of the man we know as Joseph, Jr. The ages of their children who came to Telfair County with their father, fit very well with a 1780 marriage date. Another bit of weight is added to the "Mealy Bevin" theory by the fact that this man had a granddaughter named Amelia whose family called her Mealy.

3. BYRD, a private serving under his brother Aaron in the Revolutionary War, married ZILPHA, daughter of the John Williams who is thought to be the brother of Joseph Sr. If this belief is true, this begins a pattern of first cousin marriages which included four first cousins mating within four consecutive generations.

4. WILLIAM was a private in the Revolutionary War and is presumed to have died young and unmarried.

5. PHOEBE, 1763-1842, married GEORGE BANNERMAN.

6. DAVID, 1765-1830, married ELIZABETH ANDERSON.

7. JOHN, 1768-1840, married NANCY WALLACE

CHILDREN OF JOSEPH and MEALY WILLIAMS:

1. MARY, b. 1781, died about 1858, married REDDEN RAWLINS,
Probably the son of James Rawlins, who bought land in the Rockfish Creek area of Duplin County, in 1778. Mary and Redden were married in 1804.

2. REBECCA, 1783-1880, married WILLIAM PARKER in Duplin County, N.C. in 1806.

92

3.   PHOEBE, 1785-1857, married CULLEN BONEY of Duplin County. He took part in the administration of the estate of John Boney, Jr., who is believed by some to be his father. (All the Boneys of Duplin County are descendants of Joggi Boni of Frenkendorf, Switzerland, and his wife Eva Zellar.) Cullen died in 1841, but there is no birth date on his tombstone. One source in North Carolina gives his birth year as 1797. Perhaps this isn't correct, since it makes him twelve years younger than his wife. Yet a much younger husband could help explain why she never had a child until after 1820.

4. NANCY, b. 1787, married WILLIAM WHITE.

5. JOSEPH B., b 1789, married SARAH FLETCHER. He was killed in a steamboat explosion on the Ocmulgee River in 1861.

6. DAVID J., b. 1795, married ANN _____. In 1880 she was living in Appling Co., Ga. In the home of a grandson, Garry Quinn Williams. David had died in Telfair Co., and under the terms of his will, probated in 1856, his wife was his sole heir. She was to be able to pass the property on to the children as she saw fit. The will was unsuccessfully challenged by their son-in-law Henry Wells.

7. ELIZABETH, b. 1799, married her first cousin JOHN, SON OF Byrd and Zilpha Williams. John was an officer in the Georgia Militia (Telfair County) from 1825-1829. One source erroneously states that Elizabeth married Wright Parker in 1832. That was another Elizabeth Williams who had moved with her husband to Irwin County, Ga. By 1837, while the Elizabeth, with which we are concerned, was still living as a Williams in Telfair County as late as 1860. Someone else has said, probably based on her surname never changing, that Elizabeth never married. That she had children is certain, for in 1837 her father gave "to my daughter Elizabeth Williams and her children" certain slaves. (Telfair County Deed Book K, page 195.) Marilou Smallwood, in her books, *Burch, Harrell and Allied Families*, lists a known child, Elizabeth, as a child of John. This information, along with material gathered from various census records has led this researcher to

conclude that John and Elizabeth were husband and wife. In this way, she would have been married, but her surname would be unchanged.

8. WILLIAM H., b. 1802, married CHARLOTTE _____.

KNOWN CHILDREN OF BYRD AND ZILPHA WILLIAMS:

1. JOHN married his cousin ELIZABETH WILLIAMS.

2. LAZARUS MATHIS married KATHERINE PARKER, daughter of Alexander and Anna Parker.

CHILDREN OF MARY AND REDDEN RAWLINS:

1. PRISCILLA JANE, 1802-1890, (according to her tombstone, which may be wrong for her parents were not married until 1804). She married DUNCAN CAMERON, son of Allen Cameron and Margaret Buchanan. They were buried in Telfair County's Bethelem Methodist Church Cemetery, which is commonly called Sandhill and was the burying ground for most of the Rawlinses and Camerons.

2. MATHIS, 1810-1875, married JOANNA HARRELL, daughter of William Harrell and Mary Catherine Bass, who were also former residents of Duplin County.

3. REDDEN, b. 1814, married ELIZABETH KEENE. He is reported to have died on the way home from the Civil War.

4. JAMES W., b. 1815. In 1839 he married MRS. ELIZABETH CRAVEY PARRAMORE, WIDOW OF Noah Parramore. She was much older than James, and they never had a child. (But she did bring lots of money to the marriage.) James' second wife was his cousin MARY (Polly) WILLIAMS, daughter of Joseph Gooden Williams.

5. JOSEPH THOMAS, 1818-1869, married CATHERINE (KATIE) HARRELL, sister of Joanna above. Joseph was murdered in a fight over a woman. (See page 48 in this book.)

6. AMELIA ANN, 1822-1900, married SAMUEL MCDUFFIE.

7. ISSAC, 1822-1901, married NANCY BROWN.

8. ARCADIA, who died young.

CHILDREN OF REBECCA WILLIAMS AND WILLIAM PARKER:

1. MILDRED (Milsey) MARIA, 1809-1884, married HUGH COOK. He was murdered. (See the text on court sessions.) Her second husband was HENRY CAMPBELL of Virginia.

2. WILLIAMS, b. 1811. There is no further record of him, except for his gravestone which gives no date of death.

CHILDREN OF PHOEBE WILLIAMS AND CULLEN BONEY:

1. MARY JANE, b. 1820-1900, married JOSHUA CRAVEY.

2. STEPHEN, 1823-1898, married his first cousin MARTHA WILLIAMS, daughter of Joseph B. Williams.

3. ANN ELIZA, b. 1825, married PHILLIP REAVES, son of Drury Reaves and Elizabeth Brown.

CHILDREN OF NANCY WILLIAMS AND WILLIAM WHITE:

It appears that this couple had four sons and two daughters. JOHN, LUKE, AND BRIGHTMAN were probably three of the sons. EMMALINE, who married William Smith may have been their daughter. But the only two children of whom this researcher is fairly certain are:

1. JOSEPH B., who married his first cousin EMILY WILLIAMS, daughter of John and Elizabeth.

2. ANNA JANE, who married JAMES PARKER, son of Alexander Parker and Anna Hanchey, both former residents of Duplin County.

CHILDREN OF JOSEPH B. WILLIAMS AND SARAH FLETCHER:

1. WINNIE SUE, 1826-1868, married WILLIAM LEVI (TIGER BILL) HARRELL, son of William and Mary Catherine Harrell.

2. WILLIAM F., b. 1829, married first POLLY ANN COFFEE, then MARY AMANDA BUSSEY, and thirdly FREDONIA BUSSEY.

3. MARTHA, 1831-1900, married STEPHEN BONEY.

4. ELIZA married JOHN MOBLEY.

5. JOSEPH B., JR., born 1834, married CECILIA REED. He died young after having fathered only one child, George.

6. WILEY JACKSON, B 1834, married MARY WILLCOX, REBECCA WILLCOX, and MOLLIE MIZELL.

7. THOMAS J., b. 1841, married a MRS. SHARP of Tattnall County, Ga.

CHILDREN OF DAVID J. AND ANN WILLIAMS:

1. MOLLY (Molsey), about 1822-1866. In 1835, she became the first wife of Henry Wells, son of Jeremiah Wells, who appears to be from North Carolina as is evidenced by the fact that he was a witness that Joseph Williams, Jr. fought in the Revolutionary War, when the latter applied for a pension. (There are some questions to the nationality of the Duplin County Wellses. In *Descendants of Jacob Wells of Duplin County, North Carolina*, J.W. Wells expressed the opinion that the Wells family originated in Normandy and spread from there to other parts of Western Europe. He believes that they reached North Carolina with Baron de Graffenreid's colony, as part of its Palantine component. Dr. Dallas Herring disagrees with this contention, stating that he believes they originated in the British Isles. And indeed, it is true that two of the signers of the Magna Carta had the surname Wells.)

2. A DAUGHTER, who died before 1846, was the first wife of CHARLES POWERS and had one child David W. Powers.

3. BRYANT NEWCURT, 1830-1900, He first married ANGEL QUINN, DAUGHTER OF Calvin and Teresa May Quinn. His second wife was MARGARET ANN RAWLINS, granddaughter of Mary Williams and Redden Rawlins. Bryant's name is of some interest. Bryant Newcurt (originally Newkirk) Williams was a name used both in Duplin County and in southern Georgia. The Williams sons with this name seem to be named for Bryant Newkirk, a member of a Dutch family who were early settlers in North Carolina. Bryant Newkirk's sister, Anna Jane, married Stephen Williams, grandson of Joseph

Williams, Sr. She named her son for their brother. Soon there were other Bryant Newkirk Williamses. (It is not known whether David Williams' wife Ann had a connection to the Newkirk family.) Dr. Dallas Herring, a Duplin County, N.C. historian, has wondered if the name "Bryant" was an attempt by the Newkirk family to anglicize "Barents," an old Dutch name which was the name of Bryant Newkirk's grandfather.

4.   ROBERT TIMOTHY, 1834-1892, married AMANDA QUINN, sister of the above mentioned Angel.

Both of David's sons moved to Appling County fairly soon after marrying and are buried in Zion Cemetery in Hazlehurst, Georgia. All the Wellses presently living in Telfair County are descendants of Molsey Williams and Henry Wells.

CHILDREN OF ELIZABETH AND JOHN WILLIAMS:

1.   EMILY, b. about 1822, married her first cousin Joseph B. White, son of Nancy and William.

2.   JOSEPH GOODEN, 1823-1894, married PRISCILLA PETERSON.

3.   A DAUGHTER, who died young.

4.   LUCIUS, 1834- 1894, married CATHERINE GARRISON, daughter of Darius and Sarah Harrell Garrison who both came from Duplin County. His second wife was MARGARET MCDERMID, daughter of John and Martha McDermid.

CHILDREN OF WILLIAM H. AND CHARLOTTE WILLIAMS:

About all the information on this particular branch of the family available at this time is taken from the 1850 census of Telfair County. At this time the household consisted of :

WILLIAM H. age 48

CHARLOTTE age 48

JOSEPH R. age 17

MARGARET age 14 (Author's note: She married LEVI WORRELL in 1852.)

GILBERT age 11

NANCY age 5

JOSEPH age 100

CHILDREN OF DUNCAN CAMERON AND PRISCILLA JANE RAWLINS:

1. ANDREW JACKSON, 1828-1888, married his first cousin MARGARET MARY ANN ELIZABETH CAMERON, daughter of Daniel Cameron and Isabelle McArthur.

2. MARGARET, 1830-1890, married THOMAS SHAW, son of Angus Shaw and Jane Morrison.

3. MARY E., 1833-1885, married her first cousin DUNCAN WILLIAM CAMERON (Long Duncan), son of Daniel and Isabella Cameron.

4. MARTHA, b. about 1835, married her first cousin ANDREW M. BOWEN, son of Betsey Cameron and John Berrien Bowen.

5. JOHN, 1837-1891, was second husband of his first cousin SARAH CATHERINE RAWLINS, daughter of Joseph T. and Katie Rawlins.

6. WILLIAM, 1842-1854.

7. REDDEN DUNCAN (Short Duncan), 1843-1925, married MARY ANN PARKER, daughter of Jacob Parker and Elizabeth Harrell.

CHILDREN OF MATHIS RAWLINS AND JOANNA HARRELL:

1. JAMES, 1835-1879.

2. MARY (Sis), b. about 1838, married Joseph Walker.

3. SUSAN, 1840-1919, married two brothers GEORGE BOWEN and CHRISTOPHER COLUMBUS BOWEN. (George died in the Civil War.)

4. ELIZABETH, 1843-1918, married WILLIAM HENRY HARRISON WEBB, son of Crawford Webb and Martha Miller.

5. YOUNG, about 1845-1922, married his first cousin REBECCA JANE RAWLINS, daughter of Isaac Rawlins and Nancy Brown.

6. JASPER NEWTON, 1848-1932, married MARY ELIZABETH WILLIAMS, daughter of Lucius Williams and Catherine Garrison.

7. MARGARET ANN, b. about 1849, was the second wife of BRYANT NEWCURT WILLIAMS.

8. ANNIE JANE, 1854-1939, married JOSEPH PAYNE MOORE.

9. ISABELLE, 1857-1944, married WILLIAM W. WILLIAMS (Bill Loosh), son of Lucius Williams and Catherine Garrison.

10. JOHN WASHINGTON, 1860-1934, married MELISSA (Gallie) Williams, daughter of Joseph Gooden Williams and Priscilla Peterson. In his later years he married MITTIE SHAW.

CHILDREN OF REDDING RAWLINS AND BETSEY KEENE:

1. LYDIA, b. 1842, was the second wife of FRANCIS HARRELL.

2. SARAH, b. 1845

3. JOSEPH, b. 1846

4. MARY, b. 1848, married a DOUGLAS.

5. MARTHA married a BALL.

6. REDDING, b. about 1855, married ROXIE GIBBS.

CHILDREN OF JAMES W. RAWLINS AND POLLY ANN RAWLINS:

1. MARY, b. 1862, married THOMAS FUSSELL.

2. JOSEPH, born 1865, hanged in 1906, married ANGELINE JOWERS, daughter of Jonathan Jowers and Rachel Cauley.

3. MARTHA, 1869-1943, married MATHEW BOWEN.

4. PRISCILLA ANN, 1872-1921, married WASHINGTON LEE WELLS.

CHILDREN OF JOSEPH THOMAS AND KATIE HARRELL RAWLINS:

1. MARY, 1840-1858, was the first wife of James Spires.

2. SARAH CATHERINE, 1842- 1891, married EPHRAIM YAWN, who disappeared during the Civil War. Then she married her first cousin, JOHN CAMERON.

3. NANCY JANE, 1844-1888, married her first cousin, JAMES GARRISON, son of Darius Garrison and Sarah Harrell.

4. REBECCA, b. 1846, married J. WESLEY YAWN.

5. JOHN 1848-1928 married SUSAN JANE BOWEN.

6. REDDING D., 1850-1893, married MARY SUSAN STUDSTILL.

7. JOSEPH THOMAS, JR., 1852-1925, married MARY LOU MCLEAN, daughter of John Mclean and Cornelia Shaw.

8. SUSAN ELIZABETH, 1853-1910, was the second wife of GEORGE TROUP STUDSTILL. Her second husband was W.B. LIVINGSTON.

9. FLORIDA, 1858-1902, married JAMES MAY QUINN, son of John.

10. AMANDA, 1860-1916, married W. ANDREW LOWERY.

11. MARGARET, 1862-1935, married JOSIAH WILLIAMS, son of Joseph Gooden and Priscilla Williams.

12. ANGEL, 1864-1881, was the first wife of ROBERT WILLIAMS, son of Joseph Gooden Williams.

JOSEPH THOMAS RAWLINS, SR. Had four acknowledged illegitimate children (See Telfair County Inferior Court Minutes 1857, pages 35 and 36). The children's mother was NANCY JANE PARKER, daughter of Samuel and Alice Parker from South Carolina. The Parker family lived neighbor to the Rawlins family when the 1840 census was taken. Samuel and his wife had four children, none of whom were ever married, although the two oldest girls, Polly (Pop) and Nancy Jane, both had children.

CHILDREN OF JOSEPH THOMAS RAWLINS AND NANCY JANE PARKER:

1. JAMES, b. about 1847, was married twice and both wives were named SARAH JANE.

2. ELIZA, 1852-1935, married WILLIAM HENRY CRAVEY.

3. WOOTSON, b. about 1855, married SARAH JANE HOLDER.

4. MARY ARMINTA, b. about 1856, married MARK CRAVEY and then MARK GLOVER.

CHILDREN OF AMELIA ANN RAWLINS AND SAMUEL MCDUFFIE:

1. MARY JANE, 1842-1878, was the second wife of JAMES SPIRES.

2. JAMES, b. about 1844, married JANE CRAVEY, daughter of Joshua and Mary Jane Boney Cravey.

3. GEORGIA, b. about 1846.

4. THOMAS JACKSON, b. about 1850, married ELIZA _____.

5. NANCY C., b. about 1852, married BILL CARTER.

6. SAMUEL LUKE, about 1854-1926, married ELIZABETH CRAVEY, daughter of Joshua.

7. WILLIAM, b. about 1856, married MAMIE COLEMAN.

8. DUNCAN, b. about 1859, never married.

9. JANE, b. about 1861, never married, but had three children.

CHILDREN OF ISAAC RAWLINS AND NANCY BROWN:

1. REBECCA JANE, 1850-1928, married her first cousin YOUNG RAWLINS.

2. MARK, b. about 1852 married CATHERINE (Callie) STUDSTILL, daughter of George Troup and Sarah Jane Weeks Studstill.

3. MARTHA, 1854-1889, was the first wife of M.G. FENNELL.

4. MARY, 1855-1876?

5. ENOCH, b. about 1858, married SARAH GRAHAM.

6. DAVIS, 1860-1876

7. LYDIA, 1862-1928, was the second wife of BEN WILLIAMS, son of Joseph Gooden Williams. This was a late marriage, and there were no children.

8. NANCY, b. about 1866, married CHARLIE CLEMENTS.

9. JOANNA (Jody), b. about 1868, married WILL CLEMENTS.

CHILDREN OF MILSEY MARIA PARKER COOK CAMPBELL:

FATHERED BY HUGH COOK:

1. OLIVER HUGH, b. about 1831, married REBECCA WILCOX, daughter of George and Sarah Daniel Wilcox.

2. MARIA JANE, b. about 1833.

FATHERED BY HENRY CAMPBELL:

3. WILLIAM, 1839-1883, married SUSANNAH WILCOX, daughter of Mitchell Griffin, and Martha Swain Wilcox.

4. LUKE, b. 1840, died in Fairfax, Va. In 1861.

5. GEORGE W., b. 1842, married ELIZA ENNIS.

6. REBECCA, b. 1845, married a GILMORE.

7. CHARLES WRIGHT, 1847-1926, never married.

CHILDREN OF MARY JANE BONEY AND JOSHUA CRAVEY:

1. SUSANNAH, about 1840-about 1870, married WILLIAM PARKER, son of Jacob and Elizabeth Harrell Parker.

2. CULLEN, 1842-1889, married SARAH MCLEOD, daughter of James and Caroline Rushen McLeod.

3. DAVID, B. about 1844.

4. MARTHA, b. about 1846.

5. JANE, b. about 1848, married JAMES MCDUFFIE, son of Samuel and Amelia Rawlins McDuffie.

6. ELIZABETH, b. about 1850, married SAMUEL LUKE MCDUFFIE, brother of James mentioned above.

7. JOHN, about 1857-1916.

8. MARY, b. about 1862.

9. WILLIAM, b. about 1864, married MARY SELPH.

In 1880, there were, according to the census records, several extra children in the home of Joshua Cravey. They were Louis and Wesley Cravey, grandsons, probably illegitimate children of the daughter Elizabeth; and Robert Parker, great-grandson, probably the illegitimate child of Mary Parker, granddaughter.

CHILDREN OF STEPHEN AND MARTHA WILLIAMS BONEY:

1. JOHN CULLEN, b. about 1850, married REBECCA WILCOX.

2. WILLIAM FLETCHER, 1852-1916, married MOLLY MIZELL.

3. JOSEPH JACK, 1855-1934, married his first cousin CLARA PAYNE WILLIAMS, daughter of William F. Williams and Mary Amanda Bussey.

4. WILEY M., 1858-1859.

5. REBECCA, 1861-1868.

6. ALEXANDER, 1863-1946, married REBECCA SWAIN and then POLLY BLOODWORTH.

7. ANNA, 1865-1880.

8. LUCIUS W., 1868-1958 married EMMA SWINNEY.

9. LOUIS, 1870-1872.

10. ROBERT SAXTON, 1874-1898

There is some question about the parentage of children numbers 8 and 10, according to the 1880 census of Telfair County page 1, supervisor's district 3, enumerator district 93, which is copied below.

BONEY, STEPHEN 53

MARTHA   49   WIFE

WILLIAM F.	27	SON
JOSEPH J.	25	SON
ALEX	16	SON
ANNIE	14	DAUGHTER
GIDDENS, THOMAS J.	10	BOARDER
WIMBRICK, LUCIUS	12	BOARDER
ROBERT, SAXTON	6	BOARDER

CHILDREN OF JOSEPH B. WHITE AND EMILY WILLIAMS:

1.   ELIZA, b. about 1840, married THOMAS GARRISON, son of Darius and Sarah Harrell Garrison.

2.   JAMES, b. about 1843.

3.   MARTHA, b. about 1844.

4.   MARY, b. about 1851, married J.W. STEPHENS.

5.   JOHN, b. about 1854.

6.   ANNA JANE, about 1857-1939, was the second wife for NEWTON R. WELLS, son of Henry and Molsey Williams Wells.

CHILDREN OF MOLLY J. (Molsey) WILLIAMS AND HENRY WELLS:

1.   JASPER, 1836-1901, married CATHERINE PRIEST.

2.   ELLENDER

3.   NEWTON, 1840-1911, married MARTHA_____, who died young. Then he married ANNA JANE WHITE, daughter of Joseph B. and Emily Williams White.

4.   WASHINGTON T., about 1841- about 1875. No record of marriage has been found.

5.   ANDREW JACKSON, born about 1843, died before 1880, married ROSEANNA BELLE McEACHIN, daughter of John McEachin.

6.   JEREMIAH died young.

7. ELIZABETH, b. about 1848, married GEORGE DANIEL WILCOX, had a child, Rebecca, and became a widow about 1872.

8. ANNIE, 1859-1906, married H.E. MORRIS.

CHILDREN OF BRYANT WILLIAMS AND ANGEL QUINN:

1. SARAH, b. about 1852, may have been twin to Garry.

2. GARRY QUINN, about 1852-1900, married SUSAN WILCOX, daughter of Woodson and Susannah Swain Wilcox.

3. JOHN ROBERT, 1857-1925, married ELIZABETH O. WILCOX, sister of Susan above.

4. BEULAH married JAMES REDDING.

5. DAVID JONES, b. about 1860, married MOLCY (Molly) WELLS, daughter of Jasper Wells.

6. BRYANT MORGAN, b. about 1865, married ELIZABETH PIKE.

7. MAE

8. WALTER LEE married CATHERINE WILLIAMS, granddaughter of Robert Timothy Williams, Sr.

CHILDREN OF BRYANT WILLIAMS AND MARGARET RAWLINS:

1. JAMES LATIMER, 1879-1909, married EULA COOK.

2. EUGENE married OLLIE STOWERS.

3. ANNIE, 1887-1952, married LYMAN WILCOX.

4. EDITH BRYANT, b. 1889 married ALBERT MILTON.

5. ROBERT BRYANT, 1891- 1961, married LETITIA VARN.

CHILDREN OF ROBERT T. WILLIAMS AND AMANDA QUINN:

1. ROBERT T. JR., b. about 1853, married LUCRETIA HALL.

2. ANNA

This couple had other children, but their names are not available at this time.

CHILDREN OF JOSEPH GOODEN WILLIAMS AND PRISCILLA PETERSON:

1. MARY (Polly), b. about 1842, married JAMES W. RAWLINS as his second wife.

2. JAMES K. POLK, 1845-1890, married ROXANNA FUSSELL, daughter of Jacob and Lucretia Cummings Fussell.

3. GEORGE MORRIS, 1847-1905, married MARTHA FUSSELL, sister of Roxanna mentioned above.

4. BENJAMIN, 1850-1926, married MARY MCDERMID DURR, daughter of John and Martha McDermid and widow of Dr. Michael Durr. After the death of Mary, Ben married LYDIA RAWLINS, daughter of Issac.

5. SUSAN JANIE, 1852-1911, was the first wife of DAVE WELLS, son of Jasper and Catherine Wells.

6. MOSES, 1857-1924, married MARY ANN JONES, daughter of Robert and Mary Crane Jones. His second wife was DESSIE ROBERSON.

7. ROBERT, 1860-1928, married ANGEL RAWLINS, daughter of Joseph and Katie Rawlins and, secondly, GEORGEANNA FUSSELL, daughter of Matthew and Emily Curry Fussell.

8. JOSIAH, 1865-1925, married MARGARET RAWLINS, daughter of Joseph T. and Katie Rawlins.

9. MELISSA (Gallie), 1866-1919, married JOHN WASHINGTON RAWLINS, son of Mathis Rawlins.

CHILDREN OF LUCIUS WILLIAMS
BY CATHERINE GARRISON:

1. WILLIAM (Bill Loosh), 1855-1910, married ISABELLE RAWLINS, daughter of Mathis and Joanna Rawlins.

2. MARY ELIZABETH, 1861-1937, married JASPER NEWTON RAWLINS, son of Mathis Rawlins.

3. T. JACKSON (Jack), 1863-1922, married MOLLIE CAMERON, DAUGHTER OF Duncan Cameron and Mary Parker.

CHILDREN OF LUCIUS WILLIAMS
BY MARGARET MCDERMID:

4. JOHN MORGAN, 1868-1930, married JANIE ELIZABETH (Missy) CAMERON, sister of Molly mentioned above.

5. CARRIE, b. about 1872, married DANIEL OWEN KELLY.

6. STEPHEN (Punch), b. about 1875, married LOU HULETT. His second wife was a HATTEN.

7. ARTHUR, b. about 1879, married LOLA PAULK. He died young.

8. LUCIUS (Nig) married ELOISE HARRIS. Lucius is said to be the father of a son by Mary Kerr. The child, Raz, was raised by Jack and Mollie Williams.

9. CLARENCE married TINCEY DREW.

CHILDREN OF JASPER AND CATHERINE PRIEST WELLS:

1. DAVID J., 1857-1923, married SUSAN JANIE WILLIAMS: they had one child, Collier. David's second wife was MATTIE FUSSELL, daughter of Jacob Fussell III and Mary Cravey.

2. MOLCY, b. about 1860 married DAVID JONES WILLIAMS, son of Bryant Williams and Angel Quinn.

3. JAMES, b. 1864, married MARGARET JOSEPHINE (Jo) GARRISON, daughter of Darius and Sarah Garrison.

4. WASHINGTON LEE, 1866-1935, married PRISCILLA ANN (Annie) RAWLINS, daughter of James and Polly Rawlins.

5. ROBERT, b. about 1869, was blind.

6. TALLIE J. (Tal), 1872-1956, married DRUCILLA FUSSELL. His second wife was MARY ANN SEIGLER.

7. JASPER BROOKS, 1975-1951, married CORA JANE WILLIAMS, daughter of Robert and Georgeanna Fussell Williams.

8. HENRY, 1877-1955, married DORA WILLIAMS, sister of Cora mentioned above.

CHILDREN OF GEORGE MORRIS WILLIAMS AND MARTHA FUSSELL:
1. VIOLA married DR. CHARLES FLETCHER.
2. CORA, 1872-1952. Married JOE FLETCHER and then a BURROWS.
3. BRYANT, b about 1874.
4. JOHN CRUM married MATTIE SEIGLER.
5. WILEY married JULIE PAULK.
6. LULA, 1881-1961, married RAWLEIGH BONEY.
7. MINNIE, 1884-1935, married DARSEY JONES
8. GEORGE MORRIS, 1890-1953, married ESSIE FUSSELL.
9. MATTIE married GROVER CLEVELAND WILLIAMS.

GEORGE MORRIS WILLIAMS also had an illegitimate son, ANDREW WILLIAMS, born 1864. The child's mother was Eliza White Garrison. (See page 12 of this book.)

CHILDREN OF BENJAMIN WILLIAMS AND MARY McDERMID DURR:
1. CHARLIE C. married POLLY DORMINEY.
2. BARCLAY SCOTT (Bunk) married BESSIE MIZELL.
3. WILEY married VIOLA EVERETT.
4. LEILA married JOHN C. MALOY.
5. ELLA married DR. WILLIAM DORMINEY.

CHILDREN OF ROBERT WILLIAMS AND GEORGEANNA FUSSELL:
1. GEORGE, 1882-1951, married CLAUDIA HILL.
2. ANDERSON married LUCY HARPER.
3. CORA married JASPER BROOKS WELLS.

4. DORA married HENRY WELLS.

5. EMMA married WILL BASS.

6. NEIL married ANNIE LOU KINNETT.

CHILDREN OF MOSES WILLIAMS AND MARY ANN JONES: (Not in birth order)

1. BLANEY married SALLY BRYANT.

2. ABBIE married CHRISTOPHER COLUMBUS FUSSELL.

3. MOLLIE married ELVIN YAWN.

4. SEYMOUR married MINNIE WELLS.

5. THOMAS DANIEL married GENEVA WILLIAMS, daughter of Andrew.

6. JOSEPH DAVID married EFFIE WILLIAMS, sister of Geneva above.

CHILDREN OF MOSES WILLIAMS AND DESSIE ROBERSON: (Not in birth order).

1. MYRTLE married JOHN NEWSTON SMITH and CHARLES O'KEEFE.

2. MOSES married EMILY BURKE.

3. SIKES married ESTELLE KNIGHT.

4. LOTTIE married HUGHY McDANIEL.

5. PEARL married REVELS. There was also a second marriage.

6. JANIE SUE died young.

7. CHARLIE died young.

CHILDREN OF JOSIAH WILLIAMS AND MARGARET RAWLINS:

1. WRIGHT married LEILA BOWEN.

2. LIZZY died young.

3. GARY JOE married MEXIA HEATH.

4. JOHN married ODESSA _____.

109

5. JAMES R. married RENA BOWEN.

6. LENARD

7. KINNIE JOE SEPHERS died young

CHILDREN OF MELISSA WILLIAMS AND JOHN WASHINGTON RAWLINS:

1. ANNIE JANE never married.

2. MAMIE married ANDREW SPIRES.

3. EVA married HARRY WILLIAMS.

4. MATTHEW married ANNIE TOWNS.

5. ELLA married EMBRY WALLACE.

6. BESSIE married GEORGE BASS and HARRY WILLIAMS

CRAVEY

The family we know as Cravey migrated during the early 1700's from Rascommon County, Ireland to North Carolina. At that time their name was McCravey. (See the Edgecombe County N.C. estate administration records for 1768.) So far as is known, the first of this family to arrive in the New World was Owen McCravey, Sr. The name of his first wife is not known, but he had four children by her:

1. JAMES, whose will is dated 1758, probably never married, but is said to have had an illegitimate daughter, Mary Brown.

2. PRISCILLA married to an ALLEN.

3. ANNE married to PATRICK MCKEAN.

4. HONOUR married FRANCIS ELLINOR.

After the death of his first wife Owen Cravey, Sr. married SARAH BROWN and had two sons:

1. OWEN, born 1740, married CELIA JOHNSTON. His second wife was MARY HINES, daughter of David Hines.

2. HUGH

When James Cravey died, he left a rather interesting will in which he implied that Owen, Jr. was not a Cravey. The validity of this claim is open for question, considering that James obviously did not like his stepmother, who had by this time married a Jordan. The will is copied below (including misspellings).

"Bequeath to the Parson or parsons of the Parish that is or shall come after to save the people, where the land is all my lands that was my father's in the bounds of the old Battran (patent?) That was his for an easment to the people of the parish, for a gleabe for ever - not that they should make sale of the same. MARY BROWN, my suposed (supposed) dau, 310 A bought of DRURY STOKES, 20 cattle, 100 hogs, feather bed & furn. That is my "yousing bed whereon I ly, my mear, too iron pots, half my puter case of knives & forks, ovell table, 6 chairs, iron spit, peare of sad irons, to her and her heirs lawful begotten of her body." In case of death of MARY BROWN, her part of estate shall be equally divided between my sister's chil. JEAN ALLEN, niss (niece), 100 acres bought of COLLIN WILLIAM BAKER, 20 cattle, 100 hogs, fether bed and furniture which has lately had a new tick, meare and colt, two iron pots, half my puter, case of knives and forks, 6 chears, chest that was my father's. In case of death of JEAN ALLEN without issue her part estate shall be equally divided between sister's chil. OWEN BROWN, my "spoosed" half brother, all tame bees and hives, gun, horse, all wearing clothes; HUGH CRAVEY, half Bro, 1 riffell, 2 guns and all ready money and horse. SARAH CRAVEY JORDEN, that unhappy woman–the beds she bought, 1 rugg, bed sheats, spinning wheal, linen wheel, 4 pare cards, puter dish, plate, 3 basons, box iron and heaters, cloth loom, 3 shutters, pare working bars and boxes, 3 stays and harness, pare sezors, working iron, rolling pin, chest, box trunk, too stays and harness and as for chears and hogs she has destroyed, and raised not aney, I give her 2 bedtrays, I squeare table, a pasell of stools and if this do not content her & she should sue for her 1/3, you may find recepts of dets I have paid for my father, & you will find that she has no right at all, and I order that is shall be tried by law.Exr: ROBERT WARREN, his son, KICHEN WARREN, no witnesses."

HUGH CRAVEY married twice. It is known that he had a son named HUGH, JR. His brother Owen, Jr., also had a Hugh Jr. One of the Hughes had two children who lived in Telfair County, at one time. They are:

1. JACOB, 1785-1850, married SUSANNAH PARRAMORE. He died in Coffee County, Ala.

2. ELIZABETH married NOAH PARRAMORE. Her second husband was JAMES W. RAWLINS.

CHILDREN OF OWEN CRAVEY JR. and CELIA JOHNSTON:
1. Mary, b. about 1762.
2. HUGH JR.

CHILDREN OF OWEN CRAVEY, JR. and MARY HINES:
3. JAMES died in Burke County, Ga.
4. WILLIAM never married, died in Telfair County, Ga.
5. DAVID married SUSANNA STUDSTILL, daughter of Hustus Studstill and Elizabeth Hardeman and died in Telfair County about 1848.
6. HENRY was in Montgomery County, Ga. About 1820, but they soon moved to Texas.

7 SUSANNA

8. JOSHUA married AMY STANELAND in Bulloch County, Ga. in 1817.

Shortly after the death of Owen Cravey, Sr., around 1795, his widow and children moved to Burke County, Ga. From there they scattered into parts of Georgia, Alabama, and Texas.

There were other Craveys in Telfair County in the 1800's. They are believed to be the children of the James Cravey who died in Burke County. They are:

1. JOHN, who married EFFY GRAHAM, daughter of Alexander Graham. In 1850 he was in the household of Jacob Parker. He later moved to Alabama where he died.

2. JOSHUA, who married MARY JANE BONEY. (See a list of their children in this genealogy.)

3. ESTHER, who married JACOB PARKER, SR. They lived in Burke County Georgia where their only known child, Jacob, Jr., was born. In 1834 Esther was united with the Bark Camp Baptist Church in Burke County and was dismissed by letter in 1836. It was probably at this time that she and her son moved to Telfair County. It is not entirely certain whether Jacob, Sr. came with them or whether he was already dead.

CHILDREN OF DAVID AND SUSANNA CRAVEY:

1. JOHN, 1823-1885, married ELIZABETH CAMPBELL, SARAH JANE BURNHAM, and CEALY PICKREN.

2. DAVID, JR., 1825-1906, married LYDIA STUDSTILL, daughter of William and Susanna Fletcher Studstill. His second wife was CATHERINE CAMPBELL, sister of Elizabeth mentioned above.

3. WILLIAM, b. 1828, married ELIZABETH GAINEY and moved to Turner County, Georgia.

4. MARTHA, b. 1830, married FELIX FUSSELL. Her second husband was IRA KNOWLES. She and Ira died in Polk City, Fla.

5. WINNEY, b. 1832, never married.

6. SUSANNAH married GEORGE YANCEY, SR. and had five children. She died young.

7. MARY, b. 1835, was the second wife of GEORGE YANCEY, SR.

CHILDREN OF DAVID CRAVEY, JR. AND LYDIA STUDSTILL:

1. GEORGE TROUP married ELLEN REAVES.

2. SUSAN never married.

CHILDREN OF DAVID CRAVEY JR. AND CATHERINE CAMPBELL:

3. JOHN MORRISON married LENORA McLEAN, daughter of John and Cornelia Shaw Mclean.

4. MARY, 1856-1939, married JACOB FUSSELL III, son of Jacob, Jr. and Mary Harrison Fussell.

5. LYDIA JANE, 1856-1922, married HANSFORD McLEOD, son of James and Caroline Rushen McLeod. (Note that Mary and Lydia have the same birth year. These dates came from tombstone records.)

6. SARAH

7. CATHERINE

8. LIZZIE married PEARL TATUM.

CHILDREN OF JOHN CRAVEY AND ELIZABETH CAMPBELL:

1. SUSANNAH, b. 1846, married J. BEZANT WALKER.

2. DANIEL CAMPBELL, b 1848, married ABIGAIL PICKREN, daughter of Lovett Pickren.

3. DAVID, b. 1850, married a woman who became insane. He left, supposedly to go to Texas, and was never heard from again.

4. ROBERT CHARLES, b. 1852, married MARGARET STUDSTILL, daughter of Zach and Isabel Maloy Studstill.

5. WILLIAM HENRY, b. 1854, married ELIZA PARKER, illegitimate daughter of Joseph Rawlins and Nancy Jane Parker.

6. MARGARET, 1856-1862.

7. MARY, 1858-1962.

8. JOHN JACOB, b. 1860, married MARTHA JONES, daughter of Bob Jones. His second wife was REBECCA HARRELL, only child of Francis Harrell and Miranda Webb.

9. LOCHLIN MORRIS, b. 1862, married HATTIE RIGGINS.

10. Elizabeth, b. 1867, married JOHN D. MOORE.

CHILDREN OF JOHN CRAVEY BY SARAH JANE BURNHAM.

11. MELSENA, 1871- 1873.

12. EMMA, b. 1872, married MARK GARRISON, son of James and Nancy Jane Rawlins Garrison.

13. LENA, b, 1874, married JESSE KNIGHT.

14. SON, who died as an infant.

15. DAUGHTER, who died as an infant.

CHILDREN OF JOHN CRAVEY AND CEALEY PICKRIN

Sarah Jane had a child when she married John. This boy went by the name "COOT" CRAVEY.

16. IDA married MONROE CAMERON, son of John and Sarah Catherine Rawlins Cameron.

17. BENJAMIN married MAGGIE STROM.

18. JOSEPH J. married LYDIA JANE MCLEOD, daughter of Hansford and Lydia Jane Cravey McLeod.

19. TOM married KATIE FUSSELL, daughter of Jacob III and Mary Cravey Fussell.

CHILDREN OF MARTHA CRAVEY AND FELIX FUSSELL:

1. GEORGE married MORINSEY KNOWLES, daughter of Ira and Rachel Graham Knowles.

2. CATHERINE married WILLIAM KNOWLES, brother of Morinsey mentioned above.

3. WILLIAM.

4. FELIX married LAURA GRUBBS.

5. SARAH JANE, 1860-1944, married WILLIS BAXLEY.

6. JAMES THOMAS, 1863-1932.

For children of Martha Cravey Fussell by her second husband Ira Knowles, see the Knowles family.

For more detailed and complete information on the Cravey family, consult John Head, 2838 Jody Lane, Shreveport, Louisiana, who has published a book on the Craveys. Edsel Joiner and Rembert Cravey, (both deceased), both of Milan, have also prepared a great deal of research on the Cravey family.

REA, RAY

Joseph Ray lies buried in a small cemetery on a sandy hillock way back in the woods in the China Hill Community. His burial place and his life in Telfair County are, in every way, completely different from his beginnings.

Even his name changes. He was Joseph Rea at his christening in the Beverly Massachusetts Church, which was a congregational church with the same beliefs as those in Salem and Plymouth. When Joseph died, he was a Methodist Lay Minister. Beverly was a coastal village adjacent to Salem, and until 1668, was considered a part of Salem.

Joseph Rea's colorful ancestral background and the details of how he came to Telfair County, Georgia have somewhat of a fantastic quality.

The Rea's immigrant ancestor was Daniel Rea, a seaman, who bought property in Plymouth about 1630. In 1632, he moved to Salem, left his sea-going days behind, got a land grant, and became a farmer.

Joseph Rea was descended from many of the founders of the Massachusetts Bay Colony. Woodbury, Thorndike, Ober, Elliot, Herrick,

Putnam, Trask, and Dodge were all surnames of his ancestors. And he was directly descended from Roger Conant, the founder of Salem, Massachusetts.

The Reas became members of the church in Salem Village when the people there petitioned for their own meeting house. This was the church where the Salem Witchcraft Trials began.

In fact, the posthumous testimony of Joseph Rea's ancestress, Christian Woodbury Trask, was a prime element in the conviction of Bridget Bishop, the first one hanged in the infamous trials. Mrs. Trask and Mrs. Bishop were quarreling neighbors.

In 1689, Mrs. Trask, aged 29, was found with her throat cut in three places, and her windpipe cut out. The jury ruled her death a suicide.

However, in 1692 at Bridget Bishop's trial for witchcraft, the Rev. John Hale stated, "As to the wounds that she died of, ____ I then judged and still do apprehend it impossible for her with so short a pair of scissors to mangle herself so, without some extraordinary work of the devil or witchcraft."

The jury then decided that Bridget Bishop had bewitched Christian Trask into killing herself. And she was hanged by the neck until she was dead.

Captain Joseph Rea, grandfather of the Telfair county Joseph, and who was by the time of the American Revolution, a resident of Beverly, was the local Paul Revere. Upon receiving word of the British plans for Concord, he saddled his horse and rode out to the farms, loudly proclaiming the alarm. Other members of his militia followed suit, and rode off in other directions throughout Essex County. Whether with muskets, pitchforks, or cudgels, the citizens prepared themselves.

Some of the Reas, after moving to Beverly, reverted to their sea-going genes. Gideon Ray, father of the Telfair Joseph Ray, had become quite prosperous as a ship captain. Fish, corn, potatoes, cheese, furs, whale oil, horses, and cranberries, were among the things exported.

Salt, wine, sugar, and molasses were among the many items unloaded on the return voyages.

However, there was always the danger of both the cargo and crew being captured by the French, English, Turks, and pirates flying any flag. In 1801, Captain Gideon Rea died at sea. Whether this was from enemy action or disease is not known.

In 1804, Captain Rea's widow, Abigail Thorndike Rea died of consumption. Her brother, Captain Nicholas Thorndike, was appointed guardian of Joseph Rea and his brother Gideon, Jr. Of course, since most of his days were spent at sea, his wife Mehitable Rea Thorndike (the late Captain Gideon Rea's sister) was caregiver for the boys.

Then when their Aunt Mehitable died, the boys were sent to Boston, where their older brother, William, became their guardian. William, barely of age himself, listed his occupation as "merchant." In 1811, he sold land in Beverly, belonging to his younger brothers, in order to finance their education. On the legal documents, he signed his name William Ray. This was probably when his brother Joseph changed the spelling of his surname as well.

Joseph Ray was well-educated, qualifying him as a teacher. Yet the sea drew him, and he followed the footsteps of his sea-going father. He joined the crew of his uncle Nicholas Thorndike's ship.

On one return trip from the West Indies, he became very ill as the ship approached the coast of Georgia. Fearing his death, his uncle put him ashore in Darien, Georgia to get medical care.

Whether it was because his health care was particularly skilled or because it was just not his time to die, Joseph Ray recovered. He followed the Altamaha River upstream to Appling County, where about 1841 he met and married Nancy Elizabeth Deen, daughter of Smith Deen. Their first and third children were born in Appling County and the second one in Montgomery County. Appling and Montgomery counties were quite large and joined Telfair along Telfair's southeastern border. There was no Jeff Davis County at that time. This leads one to wonder if they probably lived in what is now Jeff Davis County. Thus it was but a hop and a skip to move to Telfair County, which they did by 1846.

Joseph was a teacher and Methodist Lay Minister, and when the family moved to the China Hill Community, he bought farmland and became a farmer as well.

CHILDREN OF JOSEPH AND NANCY ELIZABETH RAY:

1. JOSEPH RAY, JR., 1842-1857.

2. NANCY ELIZABETH RAY 1843-1863.

3. WILLIAM SMITH RAY, b. 1845, died about 1863 from Civil War wounds.

4. SARAH RAY, b. 1846 married ZACH MARCHANT.

5. JOHN DEEN RAY 1850-1912 married WYLANTHA ABBOTT.

6. BENJAMIN OBERLY RAY 1852-1930 married CYNTHIA ABBOTT.

7. ALBERT THORNTON RAY 1854-1923 married FLORENCE POLLARD.

8. MARY P. (Mollie) RAY 1859-1943 married HENRY HAND.

9. GIDEON COTTER RAY, 1860-1892.

10. Joseph RAY, JR., 1863-1945 married MARY CATHERINE MCCRIMMON.

When the first Joseph Ray, Jr. died, they were so determined to have a "Joseph" that they named their last son Joseph, Jr. as well.

The remainder of the Ray genealogy in the Volume will be limited to the descendents of John Deen Ray and Benjamin Oberly Ray, who married the Abbott sisters.

CHILDREN OF JOHN DEEN AND WYLANTA RAY:

1. JOSEPH BENJAMIN RAY 1875-1944, married IDA CAULEY

2. JORDAN ABNER RAY 1878-1931, married ANNIE ONEIDA FARMER.

3. JOHN HENRY RAY 1880-1947, married MAGGIE SUE BLOODWORTH.

4. MOLLIE RAY, b. 1884, died in her twenties, unmarried.

5. NEWTON ALBERT, 1887-1979, married IDA ALICE VAUGHN.

6. N.L. born 1889, died in infancy.

7. UNNAMED INFANT

CHILDREN OF BENJAMIN OBERLY AND CYNTHIA RAY

1. NANCY ELIZABETH RAY, 1876-1964 married MORGAN LANCASTER.

2. WILLIAM WASHINGTON RAY, 1878-1958 married ADDIE MAE DAVIS (ANNIE MAE)

3. MARY ELLA , 1881-1967, married WILLIAM MALOY.

4. MINDY, 1883-1911, married SANDERS CLEMENTS. She died of typhoid fever.

5. ANNIE, 1886-1961, married OTIS MCRAE.

Sources:

History of Salem, Mass., Volume I, II, III, by Sidney Perley 1924, 1926, 1928

History of Beverly, Massachusetts by Edwin Stone 1843

Salem Village Witchcraft edited by Paul Boyer and Stephen Nissenbaum 1972

Documents copied by Beverly, Massachusetts Historical Society

Family Stories

ABBOTT

Two Abbott sisters from Laurens County married two Ray brothers from Telfair County. For the rest of their lives, they lived in the China Hill community in identical houses situated about a quarter of a mile apart.

They were daughters of Abner Abbott and his second wife, Mrs. Mary Ann (Polly Ann) Gibson. This couple had 4 children:
1. MARY, 1842-1916, married W. JOE BURGESS.
2. CYNTHIA, 1844-1930, married BENJAMIN OBERLY RAY
3. JORDAN A., 1846-1910, married MARY CHRISTIAN COUEY.
4. WYLANTA, 1848-1932, married JOHN DEEN RAY.

Mary Ann (Polly Ann) Abbott has 2 sons before she married Abner Abbott in 1841. They were James Gibson, age 15, and Francis Gibson, age 13. These boys are said to have been born in Ware County, Georgia. Diligent research has not found the names of their father, nor has the maiden name of their mother been confirmed. Although some of the Jordan Abbott's descendants say she was Mary Ann Couie (note the difference in this spelling and the spelling "Couey" by Jordan's wife.) Mary Ann (Polly Ann) Abbott was born in South Carolina.

Abner Abbott was born in Bute County, North Carolina in 1778. There is some evidence that he had a twin named Jordan who died in Mississippi in 1850. At any rate, one year after Abner Abbott was born, Bute County ceased to exist: it was divided into Franklin County and Warren County.

Abner Abbott was the son of William Abbott, the grandson of Waddington Abbott and the great-grandson of Roger Abbott, who was born about 1702 in England. William Abbott moved to Warren County, Georgia where he died about 1825.

Abner Abbott married Susan Averett in 1810 in Warren County, Georgia. There are records showing the birth of two daughters: Nancy and Susannah. Nancy married Larkin Powell. It appears that the younger daughter was Susannah, who married Mailom Stripling. (But that has not been proven.)

When Abner Abbott married the widow Gibson in Laurens County, Georgia in 1841, he was about thirty years her senior. She died in 1860, and in 1861, he married Susan Walters. She became known as "the wicked stepmother." Jordan Abbott ran away from home and lived with a son of his half-sister, Nancy Abbott Powell. Cynthia and Wylanta were more direct in their opposition: They dug her grave, but I don't believe they succeeded in running her off, because she and her husband Abner were subsequently involved in a Wilkinson County lawsuit in which they sued a woman named Love Herndon.

There are numerous family stories that Mary Ann Gibson Abbott was part Indian, but this has not been proven.

For a list of the children of Cynthia and Wylanta, see the Ray genealogy. There is more information on later generations of the Ray and Abbott family and will be shared upon request.

SOURCES:

Genida Ray Edwards

Terry Simmons

Jewelene Abbott

Allen Thomas, ex-clerk of court Laurens County, Georgia

Genealogy Depts. (1) Laurens County Library; (2) Telfair County Library; (3) Dodge County Library

Federal Census Records

Marriage Records

Court Documents in Laurens, Wilkinson, Warren Counties

Grave Markers

Several internet sources : (Descendants of Roger Abbott)
http://familytreemaker.gnealogy.com/users/a/b/b/Gary-
Abbott/ODT1-0001.html

All Bute County, North Carolina Court Minutes, 1767-79 results for
Abbott family

Moore County, Mississippi Death Certificate

DAVIS/ BOBBITT/ BUMPASS

Edgar Harris Davis was born in 1836 in Person County, North
Carolina and died in 1904 in Telfair County, Georgia. He is buried in
Sandhill (Bethelem) Methodist Church Cemetery in Telfair County,
Georgia. His tombstone says "Edker Harris Davis". However, his Civil
War records, his 1859 marriage license in Putnam County, Georgia as
well as 1850 census records in Person County, North Carolina, all state
that his name was Edward . Some folks needed spelling lessons.

Edgar Davis married Mary Frances Jones, daughter of Hezekiah and
Elizabeth Barksdale Jones.

Edgar's parents were Benjamin Davis and Barbara Bobbitt, who
were married in 1818 in Granville County, North Carolina. Person
County was later carved out of Granville County. Benjamin Davis was a
wagon maker.

Their known children were:
1. WILLIAM, b. 1821, married ELIZA BRADSHER.
2. WALKER H., b. 1828, married MARGARET JOHNSON.
3. EMILY, b. 1830, no marriage date available.
4. EDGAR/EDWARD, b. 1836.
5. MARIAH ANN, b. 1839, no marriage date available.

Edgar's mother, Barbara Bobbitt, was a descendant of William Bobbitt of Glamorganshire, Wales and his wife Joanna Sturdivent. The Bobbitt's lived in Virginia and then North Carolina. Barbara (Barbary) was said to be the daughter of Solomon Bobbitt and his wife, Honour Wiggins.

Benjamin Davis' father was probably John Davis, although other sources differ. This researcher believes that John is correct. Benjamin's mother was Elizabeth Bumpass. However one chooses to pronounce this surname, the Bumpass men were an interesting crew. They were descended from Edward Bompasse, a French Huguenot, who anglicized his name and sailed into Plymouth Massachusetts on the "Good Ship Fortune" in 1621.

The Bompass/ Bumpass family later moved to Virginia, and then to North Carolina. The latter move came because this family, along with others, rebelled at paying tithes to the Church of England. To avoid severe punishment, they accepted land in North Carolina offered by the Earl of Granville.

The Bumpass men were ferocious in fighting the British and the Tories. In 1761, one John Bumpass, (there were several) steadfastly refused to swear allegiance to Great Britain, but somehow managed to escape conviction.

The Bumpass family was partial to the names *Edward*, *Samuel*, and *John*. At one point, there were so many named "John Bumpass" that they were differentiated by descriptive nicknames. There were "Tar River John," "Deep Creek John," "Deer Heard (sic) John," and "Fighting John." Tradition states that "Tar River John I" was chained to a cart wheel by the Tories and left to die of exposure.

The Bumpass men were long-lived as a rule, and were described as being above six feet tall, and tipping the scales from 200-300 pounds and above.

THE CHILDREN OF EDGAR/EDWARD DAVIS, SR. AND HIS WIFE MARY FRANCES WERE:

1. LOUISA G. (Lou), 1860-1943, married WILLIAM THOMAS WARD.

2. WILLIAM (Will), 1863-1943, married NELL GREEN.

3. ELIZABETH (Lizzie), b. 1863, married WILLIAM SULLIVAN. Divorced

4. CORINA (Cora), b. 1869 married WILLIE S. DARDEN.

5. IDA, b. 1871 died young.

6. LELA (called Leo), b. 1874 married VAN BUREN IVEY.

7. BENJAMIN HEZEKIAH, b. 1875, married ABBIE HUNTER.

8. EDGAR HARRIS, JR. (Edd), 1876-1953 married BESSIE CRAVEY.

9. HOMER, b. 1879, died young.

10. JAMES COLUMBUS (Jim), 1881-1959 married (1) BESSIE WILLIS, (2) THELMA CANNON

11. ADDIE MAE (Annie Mae), 1884-1964 married WILLIAM WASHINGTON RAY (Billy).

Edgar/Edward Davis was said to be an American Indian. He and most of his children were dark-skinned, with straight black hair and black eyes. Three of his daughters had light hair and blue eyes. In Person County, North Carolina, where he was born, there is a small Indian tribe (Person County or Sappony Indians) whose territory spans the North Carolina/Virginia line. They have some members with blue eyes and either blond or red hair. Yet no official records have been found linking the Davis family with this tribe. Benjamin Davis and his family were always listed as living in the Bushy Fork District, which is in the opposite part of Person County from the High Plains Community where the Person County Indians live.

Their location, the absence of Indian records, and the fact that Davis was a common Melungeon name leads one to believe that Edgar Harris Davis was a Melungeon.

There is further information on Davis offspring which is available on request.

Davis/Bobbitt/Bumpass Sources:
 Family Stories
 Putnam County , Georgia Legal Records
 C.S.A. Records
 Grave Markers
 U.S. Census Records
Marriages of Granville County, North Carolina, 1753-1868 by Brent Holcomb. Publication: Genealogical Publishing Company 1981
 Davis and Shaw Families of North Carolina (internet sources)
John "Fighting John" Bumpass Sr., b. 1725 Amelia County Virginia d. 5 DEC 1812
 Benjamin Davis
(http://o2ecOa3.netsolhost.com/getperson.php?personID12923&tree= ncshawfamily)
 Descendants of William Bobbitt of Glamorganshire, Wales.
http://familytreemaker.genealogy.com/users/b/o/b/Max-
Bobbitt/BOOK-0001/0002-0001.html
 Bumpass Family from Person County, North Carolina compiled by Anne Shirley Bumpass and James Richard Townsend. Written by Robah F. Bumpass (internet source):
http://geocities.com/houghtonnance/BUMPASSFamily.htm (The Bumpass Family in America)
 Descendants of Eduod Bompasse (internet source) http://familytreemaker.com/Ronnita-Jenson
 Walter Davis who provided family genealogy material.

Ernest Ray, Jr. for a Davis Family Tree.

Marriage Records

Davis and Shaw Families of North Carolina. (internet source)

GARRISON

It is a well established fact that the only Garrison to immigrate to the newly established Telfair County was Darius. All other Garrisons in the county descend from Darius and Sarah Harrell Garrison, who married here in 1824. She was the oldest child of William and Mary Catherine Bass Harrell, who settled near Jacksonville, Georgia. Both families were former residents of Duplin County, North Carolina.

Darius was the son of Thomas and Lavinia Brock Garrison. Lavinia was the daughter of Barnet and Mary Ann Brosard Brock, who were of French descent, the name having probably been originally Braque. Barnet Brock was a hero of the American Revolution.

The ancestors of Thomas Garrison (1764-1841) are not easily provable. However, there is some circumstantial evidence.

The Garrison genealogical waters were muddied for years by the "Vanderbilt Factor." Christopher Garrison and Phoebe Vanderbilt married in Staten Island, New York a few years before Garrisons began to show up in Duplin County, North Carolina. In addition, Jedidiah Garrison, who lived in Duplin County for a few years, before ending up in Banks County, Georgia, named one of his sons "Christopher." *Voila!* The Garrisons were on the Vanderbilt family tree.

However, there are no records showing that Christopher Garrison ever moved to N.C. There are no land records, tax or jury lists, no voting or military service.

In addition, the Jedidiah/Christopher element can be explained by records from Delaware showing marriages between the Garretson/Garrison family and the Hussey family, which was quite partial to the names "Jedidiah" and "Christopher". In fact, there was a Jedidiah Garretson who lived and died in New Castle County, Delaware.

Further clouding the Garrison picture were sources which claimed that Thomas Garrison (1764-1841) was the son of Ephraim Garrison, who died in 1792. That Ephraim died young is suggested by the fact that his will described himself as being "seized by a deadly disease," and the evidence is that Ephraim's children (Mary, David, and Thomas) were still minors requiring guardians ten years after the death of their father. In addition, Ephraim lists one piece of his property as being the place "that my mother lives upon." His mother was not only still alive, but apparently still living independently.

Ephraim did have a brother named Thomas, who served as one of the co-executors of the will. This brother was almost certainly the Thomas who married Lavinia Brock in 1793. Legal documents show that they had a sister Elizabeth, who married William Merrill. After the death of her husband, she moved to Effingham County, Georgia from whence location she sold property in Duplin County. Darius Garrison, who was in Effingham County at that time, was almost certainly brother to Elizabeth Thomas, and Ephraim. (For many years, Thomas' son Darius, living in Telfair County, Georgia, made annual trips to Effingham County to visit his "Uncle Darius".)

There were a number of other Garrison men living in Duplin County during the latter part of the 1700's: Adonijah, Ebenezer, John James, and Jedidiah. It is not clear exactly if or how they were kin to Thomas, but they probably were. The others either died or moved, and he was the only one who lived a long life in Duplin County.

What was the Garrison's country of origin? Actually, they came from several places. They appear to have been perennial religious refugees, fleeing here and there to escape Catholic persecution. They were found in Cornwall, Yorkshire, Scotland; fled to France during Queen Mary's reign; then on to Holland after the French King Henry, went on the rampage. Some of them then sailed to the New World.

Lysbeth (Elisabeth) Hendriksz (Hendricks), reportedly the widow of Garret Janszon, landed in Delaware in 1662, along with her two sons. (Note: The Dutch used a patronymic system of choosing surnames: they added an affix derived from a paternal ancestor's name. Thus Garret Janszon's sons were surnamed Garretson. A system in which husbands and wives, and their offspring had different surnames was outlawed by the British when they gained authority over Dutch citizens. And those with Dutch names often anglicized their surnames. Thus Garretson would become Garrison or Garrason.)

The Garretson brothers swore allegiance to the British Crown in 1683. Paul, whose line will be followed in this paper, married Elizabeth Harris. They had a son, John, who was the third husband of Elizabeth Peterson Joranson Cock Garretson. She was the daughter of Samuel and Brita Andersson Petersson, who were active in the Old Swedes Trinity Church in New Castle County Delaware.

Elizabeth was already pregnant when she married John Garretson. Their son Thomas was baptized in 1730, according to Holy Trinity (Old Swedes) Church Foundation records, as well as information from The Swedish Colonial News (Volume 3, Number 6, Spring 2007). Those sources also document Thomas' marriage to Jane Ferris in 1754. After their marriage, Thomas and Jane seem to disappear from Delaware records.

In 1765, Thomas Garrison, mariner, bought land in Duplin County, N.C. After that, he disappeared from record. However, in 1783, a Jane Garrison paid taxes in Duplin County. If she was not Thomas' wife/widow, then who was she? Research has not uncovered any reasonable suggestion about who else she could be.

The correct spelling of the Garrison/Garrason name has been the subject of much debate. Some insist that Garrason is the only correct spelling. As late as the civil war, military records of the sons of Darius Garrison give a mixed picture. Those recording muster rolls and other documents, sometimes used one spelling and sometimes another. And when Levy entered the Confederate Army, he signed his name "Levy Garrason." And then there are those who declare that they have always been Garrisons, and they will remain that way regardless of how their name is supposed to be spelled.

CHILDREN OF THOMAS AND LAVINIA BROCK GARRISON:

1. EPHRAIM married MARGARET CARR. He died in 1829.

2. DARIUS, who married SARAH HARRELL in Telfair County, Georgia in 1824, died in the 1860's. His wife's parents were William Harrell and Mary Catherine Bass, former residents of Duplin County.

3. ELIZABETH married AMOS KILPATRICK.

4. MARY married MERRELL WILLIAMS. They moved to Lee County, Georgia.

5. DAVID B., Died at age 24.

6. JAMES married MARY CATHERINE WILLIAMS. They lived in New Hanover County, North Carolina.

7. PENELOPE married JAMES WILLIAMS.

8. SARAH married WILLIAM BOSTICK, and died thirteen months later.

9. THOMAS, JR. Died at age 16.

10. CATHERINE married JOHN DOBSON.

CHILDREN OF DARIUS AND SARAH HARRELL GARRISON

1. JOHN, 1827-1862, John died of dysentery shortly after entering the Civil War.

2. LAVENIA, 1829-1898, was the second wife of ZIBIA STUDSTILL, son of William and Susannah Fletcher Studstill.

3. WILLIAM, 1830-1857.

4. THOMAS, 1832-1872, married ELIZA WHITE, daughter of Joseph B. and Emily Williams White.

5. CATHERINE, b. 1834, was the first wife of LUCIUS WILLIAMS.

6. JAMES, 1840-1886, married his first cousin NANCY JANE RAWLINS, daughter of Joseph and Katie Harrell Rawlins.

7. LEVY, 1842-1917, married LYDIA HULETT.

8. MARY ANN (Polly Ann), 1844-1924, married JESSE JONES, son of Robert and Mary Crane Jones.

9. DARIUS, 1846-1904, married MARGARET GRIMES, daughter of John.

10. CAROLINE, b. 1851, was the second wife of a JAMES WILLIAMSON, JR. She had one child Lillian who was born before she married Williamson.

11. MARGARET JOSEPHINE married JAMES WELLS.

CHILDREN OF LAVENIA AND ZIBIA STUDSTILL:

1. SARAH, b. about 1859, married WILLIAM WOOTEN.

2. INFANT, who died in 1859.

3. ELIZA, 1861-1917, married A.A. MCLEAN in 1884.

4. INFANT SON, born and died in 1862.

5. ZIBIA, 1863-1865.

6. JOANNA, 1865-1945, married MURDOCK ODOM.

7. INFANT DAUGHTER , born and died in 1868.

ZIBIA STUDSTILL HAD THE FOLLOWING CHILDREN BY HIS FIRST WIFE SARAH JANE SHAW, daughter of Angus and Jane Shaw:

1. JONATHAN, b. about 1843, married SARAH JANE MCDUFFIE.

2. SUSANNAH, b. about 1845, married JOHN H. BOWEN.

3. CORNELIA, b. about 1847, married JASPER POWELL.

4. NANCY, b. about 1849, married A. D. POWELL.

5. CATHERINE, b. about 1851, married JOHN WEEKS and then ROBERT POWELL.

6. WILLIAM, b. about 1855, married his first cousin SERENA MCLEAN, daughter of John and Cornelia Shaw McLean.

CHILDREN OF THOMAS GARRISON AND ELIZA WHITE:

1. WILLIAM, 1860-1918, married his first cousin MARY JONES, daughter of Jesse and Polly Ann Garrison Jones.

2. ROBERT, 1866-1938, married MARY (Molly) PRIDGEN.

3. MARTHA, b. about 1867, married W.L. BRENT.

4. ELWOOD COHEN was born about 1870, died about 1903. He had one daughter, but the name of his wife is unknown.

5. MARY, 1874-1906, married JOHN KELLY. She was always thought of as a Garrison, but Telfair County Inferior Court records show that she was not born until two years after the death of Thomas Garrison. So the name of her father is unknown.

Eliza White Garrison also had another illegitimate child. She had an affair with her young first cousin, George Morris Williams, while her husband was fighting in the Civil War. When George Williams was 16 years old, his and Eliza's son Andrew was born. When Thomas Garrison died in 1872, Eliza sent Andrew to live with his natural father. The child was known as a Williams for the rest of his life.

CHILDREN OF JAMES AND NANCY JANE RAWLINS GARRISON:

This couple was first cousins, their mothers being daughters of William and Mary Catherine Bass Harrell.

1. JOHN, 1868-1881, died of typhoid fever

2. JOSEPH MARK, 1870-1934 (not correct in text), married EMMA CRAVEY, daughter of John Cravey and Sarah Jane Burnham.

3. JOSEPH THOMAS (Joe), about 1872-1928, married ALICE ATKINSON, divorced after a short time, then he married SALLY TOWNS.

4. LEVI (Levy), 1877-1953, married CAROLINE CRAVEY, daughter of William Henry and Eliza Parker. Eliza was the daughter of J.T. Rawlins and Nancy Jane Parker. Nancy Jane Rawlins Garrison (called Dean) told her children that, though her husband was her first cousin

132

and they grew up about 10-15 miles apart, they never met until after he came home from the Confederate Army. "Besides," she said, "after the war, men were scarce."

5. ANDREW, 1880-1959, married FRANCES WILLIAMS, daughter of Oliver Williams.

6. SALLY, 1882-1953, married George Vickery.

CHILDREN OF LEVY AND LYDIA HULETT GARRISON:

1. WILLIAM, 1877-1942, married (1) MARY STEVERSON, (2) CHARLOTTE WALL

2. DAVID LEE, 1887-1951, married to LOLLIE MCLENDON.

3. LOLA MAE, 1889-1925, never married.

4. CARRIE, 1891-1974, never married.

5. JOHN HENRY (Bud), 1893- married EDNA BOWEN. He died in Connecticut.

6. BESSIE LEE, 1895-1967, married FRANK MORRIS WELLS.

CHILDREN OF JESSE AND POLLY ANN GARRISON JONES:

1. SARAH married LEE ANDREW TILLMAN.

2. MARY, 1870-1956, married WILLIAM GARRISON, her first cousin.

3. WILLIAM, 1874-1948, married his first cousin DELLA JONES, daughter of Middleton and Mary Jane Booker Jones.

4. WALTER (M.D.), 1876-1902, married NEAL LOWE.

5. ANDREW (M.D.), 1879-1962, married LOLA WILLIAMS, daughter of Andrew Williams and Arcadia Dopson.

6. CHARLIE married SARAH ROBERSON.

7 STEPHEN, 1884-1949, married SALLY FLETCHER, granddaughter of George Morris Williams and Martha Fussell.

CHILDREN OF DARIUS GARRISON AND MARGARET GRIMES:

1. JOHN W., b. 1870, married ANNIE PRIDGEN.

2. WILLIAM THOMAS, 1873-1876.

3. ANNIE, b. 1874, married GEORGE MCMILLIAN.

4. DAVID DARIUS, b. 1876, married MATTIE LEWIS.

5. JAMES, b. 1878, married SUSAN MCINNIS.

6. LEVY, 1881-1882.

7. CHARLIE WARREN, b. 1883, married VIOLA LEE WILLIAMS.

8. SARAH LAVINIA, b. 1886, married GEORGE FRANKLIN BARNES.

9. WILEY, b. 1888, married SUSANNA WILLIAMS.

10. DANIEL WEBSTER, b. 1891, married ALICE KATE DORMINEY

CHILDREN OF JAMES AND JOSEPHINE GARRISON WELLS:

1. EULA married ULMA BASS.

2. CATHERINE (Kate) married ED CRENSHAW.

CHILDREN OF JOSEPH MARK AND EMMA CRAVEY GARRISON:

1. BESSIE, 1894-1974, married WILL PATTERSON.

2. WILLIAM HENRY, 1898-1975, married LOUISE BONEY.

3. HATTIE, 1900-1994, married E.C. COPELAND.

4. LOCKE, b. 1902, married (1) DOVIE ANDERSON, (2) PAULINE TOWNS PATTERSON

5. DYAL, b. 1905, married CASSIE CHAMBERS.

6. STEWART, b. 1907, married NELLIE BOB CRAVEY.

7. RUTH, b. 1910, married JESSE SAWYER.

8. EMMA LOUISE, 1912-1968 married COSBY POWELL.

CHILDREN OF LEVI (LEVY) AND CAROLINE CRAVEY GARRISON:

1. EVA, 1902-1983, married J. ARNOLD PEEL.

2. H. MORGAN, 1905-1970, married MINNIE WALKER.

3. INFANT SON born and died April 9, 1907.

4. LEVI SAXTON, 1908-2001, married LULA MAE RAY.

5. MARY, 1911-1975, married ROBERT PARKER.

6. BROADUS, b. 1914-1997, married WYNELLE CLAXTON.

7. HARRY, b. 1917-1998, married (1) HELEN WARE, (2) LILLIAN _____ SMITH, (3) SALLY YAWN PARKER.

8. ERMA, 1920-2001, married (1) KENNETH SEARS, (2) BEN Y. STEPHENSON

JOSEPH THOMAS GARRISON (Joe) AND SALLY TOWNS had one daughter named Mary.

CHILDREN OF ANDREW AND FRANCES WILLIAMS GARRISON (not necessarily in birth order):

1. RAZ married LUCILLE BROWN.

2. ROZZIE married BRUCE BERRY.

3. MARY LEE married WOODROW IVEY.

4. JAMES (Jim) married (1) MARIE HILLIARD, (2) WILLENE CALDWELL.

5. LUVENIA died young.

6. EDNA died young.

7. MERLE married GERALDINE BERRY.

LIST OF CHILDREN OF GEORGE AND SALLY GARRISON VICKERY ARE NOT AVAILABLE AT THIS TIME.

GARRISON SOURCES:

Holy Trinity (Old Swedes) Church Foundation, Wilmington, Delaware

1693 Church Census Records (Crane Hook Congregation 1693 Census)

Hussey/Garretson (internet source):
http://genforum.genealogy.com/hussey/messages/1213.html Re:
Hussey m James Garretson says 1740 Delaware census.

The Swedish Colonial Society internet publication website:
http://www.colonialswedes.org/Forefathers/SamuelPetersson.html as
originally published in Swedish Colonial News Volume 3, Number 6
(Spring 2007).

Ancestors of Mary Lou Bagwell internet site:
http://familytreemaker.genealogy.com/users/e/m/b/Walter-Alan-
Embrick/GENE3-0025.html

    Grave Markers

    CSA Military Records

    Telfair County Library

    Nell Davis Harris

    Cecil Calder Garrason

    Family Stories

    U.S. Census Records

JONES

The Jones Family which settled near Jacksonville, Georgia about 1835 was headed by ROBERT W. And MARY (Molcy) CRANE JONES. Robert was from Charleston, S.C. His father's name is unknown to this writer, but his mother was Margaret. When she died, she left stock in trust for him, the interest of which he could use for the support of his family. But he was not to sell or mortgage it. A quit claim deed was signed by his brother William Jones, and his sisters, Elizabeth Disher, and Ann Seamore. (See Telfair County Deed Book J, page 127.)

CHILDREN OF ROBERT AND MARY CRANE JONES:

1. ELIZA, 1837-1924, married HENRY FUSSELL. This is believed to be Henry Harrison who took the surname of his stepfather Jacob Fussell, Jr.

2. ROBERT, b. about 1839, married MARY ANN BOWEN.

3. WILLIAM, b. about 1841, died in the Civil War.

4. JESSE, 1844-1917, married MARY ANN GARRISON, daughter of Darius.

5. LEONARD P., b. about 1845, married MARY EUGENIA DOPSON WILSON, daughter of Alexander Dopson, and widow of William Wilson.

6. MIDDLETON, 1848-1918, married MARY JANE BOOKER, daughter of Charles Booker and Margaret Jane Graham Booker. When Mary Jane was a small child, her mother was declared insane. Isabelle Graham Larkey, sister of Margaret Jane, raised her sister's child.

7. MARY, 1852-1892, was the first wife of MOSES P. WILLIAMS, son of Joseph Gooden Williams.

For the children of Jesse and Mary Ann Jones, see the Garrison Family.

For the children of Mary Jones and Mose Williams, see the Williams Family.

KNOWLES

ROBERT KNOWLES, who lived in the Rockfish Creek area of Duplin County, N.C., died testate in 1792. His heirs were his wife Elisabeth, and sons Emanuel, James, Francis, and William. EMANUEL and his wife ANN WILLIAMS married in Duplin County in 1812. David Williams furnished the marriage bond, but his relationship to the bride, if any, is unknown.

Emanuel and Ann moved to the Telfair-Appling County area about the time that so many others left North Carolina. There were four Knowles men who married in Telfair County in the early 1830's. They are believed to be the sons of Emanuel and Ann Williams Knowles and are listed below:

1. IRA married RACHEL GRAHAM.
2. WILLIAM married LUCRETIA FUSSELL, daughter of Benjamin and Lucretia Fussell.
3. BYRD married CHARITY JACKSON.
4. JOHN married SHEALEY TULLIS.

By this time Ann had already died, and EMANUEL had married MARGARET MERRITT in 1830. He had children by her and lived the rest of his life in the Coffee County, Georgia area.

CHILDREN OF IRA AND RACHEL KNOWLES:
1. NANCY (or KANEY), b. about 1833. She may have been Rachel's child before she married Ira. (They were married in 1835.) Her husband may have been JAMES A. ROBINSON (or ROBERSON), but that is not certain.
2. DAVID, 1835-1907, married SUSAN BROCK.
3. WILLIAM, b. about 1838, married CATHERINE JANE FUSSELL, daughter of Felix and Martha Cravey Fussell.

4. MORINSEY, b. about 1842, married GEORGE FUSSELL, brother of Catherine Jane mentioned above.

5. MARY, b. about 1844. Her husband may have been JOHN ROBERSON.

6. CORNELIUS (Neil).

After the death of Rachel, IRA married MARTHA CRAVEY FUSSELL, widow of Felix. Their children were:

1. JOHN, 1867-1922, married HARLINA WILLIAMS.

2. JAMES, b. 1872, married CAROLINE ROBERTS AND CALLIE WALKER.

3. MARTHA, 1873- 1963, married WILLIAM BRYANT.

CHILDREN OF DAVID KNOWLES AND SUSAN BROCK:

1. CENA, b. about 1860-1861(?) (There are no dates on her tombstone, but she was not present in the 1860 census. However, the 1870 census lists her as being 13.) She married WILL HARRISON.

2. REUBEN, 1860-1936, married WINNIE WILLIAMS, daughter of Daniel and Elizabeth Moore Williams.

3. NANCY, 1862-1953, married ANDREW JACKSON WATSON.

4. WILLIAM D., b. about 1863.

5. RACHEL, about 1867-1941, married J.B. BRILEY. (The census record and her tombstone disagree on her birth date.)

6. SUSAN E., b. about 1871.

7. CAROLINE JANE, b. about 1878, married LOUIS LEWIS.

Another branch of the Knowles Family, also descended from Robert Knowles of Duplin County, came to Telfair County a bit later. R. R. (Bob) KNOWLES came from North Carolina to Twiggs County, Georgia where he married JANE WILLIAMS, and then moved on to Telfair County. Bob's grandfather was said to be a grandson of Robert Knowles of Duplin County.

CHILDREN OF BOB AND JANE KNOWLES:

1. JOHN JOEL, 1882-1967, married LULA WHITE.

2. PHOEBE married MAC MCMURPHY and JOE WATSON.

3. JAMES ROBERT married MALINDA TOWNS, who had first been married to G.D. CONLEY.

4. HATTIE married JOE MCLEOD.

FUSSELL

Before 1832, the Fussell family began its sojourn in this area with the arrival of Benjamin Fussell and his wife Lucretia, along with all their children. Benjamin and Elizabeth Fussell had lived in the Rockfish Creek area of Duplin County, North Carolina. Benjamin and Elizabeth had two known sons, Benjamin Jr. and John.

CHILDREN OF BENJAMIN, JR. AND LUCRETIA FUSSELL:

1. JACOB married ESTHER WILLIAMS, daughter of Aaron Williams. His second wife was LUCRETIA CUMMINGS.

2. ELIZABETH married DAVID COLLINS.

3. WILLIAM married twice. His first wife may have been a STUDSTILL, His second wife was MRS. TABITHA GREEN VANN.

4. MORRIS appears in Marion County, Georgia by 1860.

5. JAMES C. was probably a twin to John. He married SALLY PARKER, daughter of Alexander and Anna Hanchey Parker.

6. JOHN married CATHERINE GIDDENS.

7. ARNOLD BENJAMIN married MARY_____.

8. NANCY married MICHAEL WELLS. They moved to Texas.

9. LUCRETIA married WILLIAM KNOWLES.

CHILDREN OF JACOB FUSSELL BY ESTHER WILLIAMS:

1. BENJAMIN

2. MARY married ABRAHAM CRUM.

3. DAVID

4. JOHN

5. ENOCH

6. CATHERINE married JAMES MURPHY.

7. BYRD married ELIZABETH HUNTER.

8. JACOB married MARRY JANE HARRISON and MARTHA LOVADAH CAMERON BRANTLEY.

9. JAMES

10. STEPHEN MILLER

11. ESTHER

12. AARON

13. BONEY married RHODA WHITLEY.

14. NANCY

CHILDREN OF JACOB FUSSELL AND LUCRETIA CUMMINGS:

1. LUCRETIA married her first cousin, ANDERSON FUSSELL, son of William.

2. SUSANNAH married WILEY WHITLEY.

3. ROXANNA married JAMES K.P. WILLIAMS.

4. MARTHA married GEORGE M. WILLIAMS, brother of James above.

CHILDREN OF JOHN FUSSELL AND CATHERINE GIDDENS:

1. FELIX married MARTHA CRAVEY.

2. THOMAS OLIVER married SARAH FLETCHER.

3. TIMOTHY married CHARLOTTE PASSMORE.

4. JOHN married DELILAH BROWN. They were divorced after many children, and he remarried.

FOR CHILDREN OF FELIX FUSSELL, SEE THE CRAVEY FAMILY.

CHILDREN OF THOMAS OLIVER FUSSELL AND SARAH FLETCHER:

1. THOMAS FLETCHER married MAGGIE MALOY.
2. ELIZABETH
3. GEORGEANNA
4. MARTHA JANE married LUTHER FUSSELL, a descendant of Benjamin Fussell's brother, John.
5. JOHN W. married CORNELIA GASQUE.
6. JAMES
7. B.O. married CLAUDIA DABNEY.
8. C.W.
9. HENRY
10. SIDNEY

CHILDREN OF JACOB FUSSELL JR. AND MARY JANE HARRISON:

1. ESTHER
2. MARY
3. JOHN
4. JACOB married MARY CRAVEY, daughter of David Cravey, Jr.
5. GEORGEANNA

Mary Fussell had a child, Henry Harrison, who adopted the surname Fussell.

CHILDREN OF JACOB FUSSELL, JR. AND LOVADAH CAMERON BRANTLEY:

1. SUSIE married ALBERT SAULS.
2. ALEXANDER
3. CHARLIE

Much more on the Fussell family is available both from this author and from Catherine Fussell Wells, who may be contacted through the Satilla Regional Library in Douglas, Georgia.

ACKNOWLEDGEMENTS
CREDIT WHERE CREDIT IS DUE

My thanks to the following resources:

Dodge County Library in Eastman, Georgia; Telfair County Library in McRae, Georgia; Laurens County Library in Dublin, Georgia; Satilla Regional Library in Douglas, Georgia; and Washington Memorial Library in Macon, Georgia. All provided valuable material for this volume.

Court records in pertinent counties in Georgia and North Carolina added to these resources.

Historical Societies in Duplin County, North Carolina and Essex County, Massachusetts were kind enough to answer a number of questions and send copies of material for which this researcher never thought to ask.

Holy Trinity (Old Swedes) Church Foundation in Wilmington, Delaware also sent valuable copies and answered questions.

Books of interest were *Georgia's Black Book: Morbid, Macabre and Sometimes Disgusting Records of Genealogized Value* by Robert Scott Davis, Jr. and *Descendants of Jacob Wells, Duplin County, North Carolina* by J.W. Wells. Catherine Wells' writings on the Cravey and Fussell Families were also useful. The three volumes of the *History of Salem, Massachusetts* by Sidney Perley and the *History of Beverly, Massachusetts* by Edwin Stone provided invaluable information. J.N. Talley's *Dodge Lands and Litigation* provided documentation on the timber wars.

Allen Thomas, retired Clerk of Court in Laurens County, Georgia, was very kind and helpful in the search for the truth.

Various internet pages were useful as well. Sometimes internet links expire, so the reader is encouraged to search for them again if necessary.

Conversations with cousins whom I had never met before filled in many gaps in my family knowledge. Walter Davis and Nell Davis Harris are kind cousins always willing to help.

Many thanks to the late J.D. Williams for giving me the ancestry of Andrew Williams and to Myrtle Knight for asking a pertinent question on that family line.

Most important of all, I give heart-felt thanks to my dad, L. Saxton Garrison. Sr. He took me on "strolls", which are a lot better than walks. As we strolled through the woods, he filled my head with history and fascinating tales.

ABOUT THE AUTHOR

Addie Garrison Briggs grew up on a farm four miles south of Milan, Georgia, in the midst of the South Georgia wiregrass territory. She first attended Progress School near Midway Church and later graduated from Milan High School. She graduated from Asbury College in Wilmore, Kentucky with majors in History and Elementary Education. In 1969 she moved with her young family back to the country outside Milan.

She and her husband live on the original site of Camp Six of the Dodge Lumber Company, which was a thriving workplace during the time that the virgin timber was being harvested in the late nineteenth century.